FREEDOM
A Step-by-Step Guide to Wealth and Financial Independence

By

Dr. Cedric B. Howard

Freedom: A Step-by-Step Guide to Wealth and Financial Independence
Copyright © 2024 by Dr. Cedric B. Howard
All rights reserved.

This book is a work of nonfiction. While the information provided is based on research and personal knowledge, all scenarios, examples, and characters mentioned in this book are used for illustrative purposes. Any resemblance to actual events, people, or situations is purely coincidental.

ISBN: E-Book: 978-1-964687-97-1
         Paperback: 978-1-964687-98-8
         Hardcover: 978-1-964687-99-5

First Edition: November, 2024

Disclaimer

Freedom: A Step-by-Step Guide to Wealth and Financial Independence is intended for informational and educational purposes only. The content in this book does not constitute financial, legal, or investment advice. Readers are encouraged to consult with qualified financial advisors, legal professionals, or tax experts before making decisions related to financial planning, investing, or any other aspects of personal finance.

While every effort has been made to ensure the accuracy of the information provided, the author and publisher make no representations or warranties regarding the accuracy, completeness, or suitability of the content for any particular purpose. Financial markets and personal finance strategies are subject to change, and the results of any financial decisions are not guaranteed.

The examples, strategies, and methods described in this book are illustrative and may not be appropriate for every reader's individual financial situation. Any actions taken by the reader based on the information in this book are solely at the reader's discretion and risk. The author and publisher assume no responsibility or liability for any financial losses, damages, or outcomes resulting from the use or misuse of the information provided.

By using this book, readers acknowledge and accept that personal finance is inherently complex and unique to each individual. Readers are encouraged to seek independent advice and take into account their own goals, financial circumstances, and risk tolerance.

Table of Contents

Dedication and Acknowledgements

This book is dedicated to those who have shaped my journey toward financial literacy and empowerment.

To Mr. Isaac Lightfoot, my DECA teacher in high school, whose guidance introduced me to the world of financial literacy. It was through his lessons on budgeting, the Rule of 72, stocks, and investing that I first learned the foundational principles of managing money. I will always remember his teaching of the poem Don't Quit, which we had to memorize as part of the DECA curriculum—*"When things go wrong as they sometimes will... You must not quit."* Those words became more than just a mantra; they served as a reminder that perseverance is key in both business and life.

My experience in DECA (Distributive Education Clubs of America) was my first real exposure to the concepts of business, entrepreneurship, and financial management. It was during this time that I understood the power of financial knowledge—not just for personal success, but for making a positive impact in the world of business. The competition, the teamwork, and the challenges of DECA helped me build a strong foundation for the future.

To Charlie Cook and Mouleen Cook, who continued to nurture my financial education during my young adult years while I was a doctoral student in Memphis. Your guidance was instrumental in deepening my understanding of advanced financial concepts and investment strategies, further shaping my journey toward financial literacy.

And to all those who dare to embrace the future of finance—those who seek to understand the intricacies of wealth-building, navigate the ever-evolving financial landscape, and pass on the torch of financial literacy to future generations—this book is for you.

May the lessons within these pages inspire you to take control of your financial destiny, just as the teachers, mentors, and experiences in my own life have inspired me.

Preface

In an era defined by rapid technological advancements, the financial landscape is undergoing a profound transformation. Artificial intelligence (AI) is no longer a futuristic concept; it is a powerful force reshaping the way we invest, manage our finances, and plan for the future. This book aims to demystify the world of AI in finance and empower individuals to harness its potential for personal wealth creation.

We stand at a pivotal juncture where the intersection of technology and finance holds immense promise. AI offers unparalleled opportunities to streamline investment processes, enhance decision-making, and democratize access to financial services. However, navigating this uncharted territory requires a clear understanding of the tools, strategies, and ethical considerations involved.

This book serves as a comprehensive guide, providing both theoretical knowledge and practical insights into the world of AI-driven personal finance. It is designed for individuals of all financial backgrounds, from beginners seeking to enter the investment world to seasoned investors looking to refine their approach.

We invite you to embark on this journey of discovery, where you will explore the latest advancements in AI-powered financial technologies, learn how to leverage these tools effectively, and gain the knowledge and confidence to make informed investment decisions that align with your financial goals.

Chapter – 1:
Introduction – The New Path to Financial Independence

Achieving financial independence is a goal that resonates with almost everyone. Who doesn't want the freedom to pursue their passions, choose their paths, and live without financial worry? However, the journey to financial independence can often feel elusive or daunting, especially in an era of rapid technological change and evolving financial landscapes. But here's the good news: technology, particularly Artificial Intelligence (AI), is not only reshaping global industries but also redefining how we approach personal finance. This book is your guide to understanding and harnessing this powerful tool to build wealth and achieve a sustainable, financially independent lifestyle.

Financial independence isn't just about accumulating wealth; it's about building a life where your finances support your freedom, security, and aspirations. The difference between those who reach financial independence and those who only dream of it often comes down to taking consistent action, staying informed, and using the best tools available. Today, AI is one of those tools—a revolutionary force that's leveling the playing field in personal finance. This book will show you how to make AI your ally, regardless of your starting point, background, or financial knowledge.

For young adults and aspiring entrepreneurs, the stakes feel higher than ever. The costs of education, housing, and even starting a business can be overwhelming. But with the right strategies and technology, financial independence is achievable, no matter your current circumstances. This book is designed to simplify the journey, cutting through financial jargon and focusing on actionable steps. From understanding your cash flow to investing confidently, you'll learn to leverage AI-driven tools to guide your financial decisions and maximize your resources.

Why AI? Traditionally, wealth-building was the domain of financial experts, brokers, and advisors—services that often come with hefty fees. AI, however, opens the doors to everyone by providing access to powerful, data-driven insights and personalized financial strategies. With the click of a button, you can receive tailored advice that adapts to your specific goals, track your spending in real-time, invest in diversified portfolios, and even analyze market trends without spending hours doing research. In essence, AI brings the expertise of an entire finance team into your pocket.

Throughout this book, you'll discover that financial independence is as much about mindset as it is about money. We'll tackle myths around wealth-building, introduce you to simple tools that make big differences, and empower you to take control of your financial journey. Embracing a proactive mindset is critical, and each chapter will encourage you to make small, practical changes that compound over time.

Starting with an honest assessment of your current financial status, you'll learn how to set realistic goals that align with your personal values. Once you've established a foundation, you'll dive into budgeting strategies, debt management, and investing—all through the lens of AI's game-changing capabilities. Whether you're looking to save for a specific goal, create passive income streams, or diversify your investments, AI can simplify and enhance each step.

With AI in your financial toolkit, you're not just managing money—you're maximizing its potential. This book will guide you through the essential steps of building wealth in a way that aligns with today's fast-paced, tech-driven world. Each chapter is designed to build upon the last, giving you a structured approach to achieve financial independence, even if you're starting from scratch.

"Think of AI as your financial coach, always a step ahead."

One of the most powerful aspects of AI is its ability to make financial planning accessible to everyone. You don't need to be a seasoned investor or have an economics degree to benefit from these tools. AI tools can monitor spending habits, suggest budgeting improvements, recommend investment options based on your risk tolerance, and help manage debt with precision. By embracing these tools, you'll not only take control of your finances but also gain insights that might have been previously out of reach.

Imagine having a financial advisor in your pocket, working 24/7.

That's what AI brings to the table.

Financial independence, at its core, is about empowerment. As you progress through the chapters, you'll learn to make decisions based on data and trends rather than guesswork. This data-driven approach will help you sidestep common pitfalls and give you the confidence to take actionable steps toward financial freedom.

With every decision backed by data, you're not just planning; you're building a legacy.

Imagine feeling secure in your choices, knowing they're backed by real-time information and intelligent analysis. This is what AI offers—a clarity that empowers you to make informed decisions and a roadmap that guides you toward your goals.

But beyond the tools and techniques, this book is about a mindset shift. True financial independence requires a commitment to continuous improvement, self-discipline, and a willingness to adapt.

Your money journey is not just numbers; it's a mindset.

The financial landscape is constantly evolving, and AI is only the beginning of the digital revolution in personal finance. By adopting the strategies outlined in this book, you'll not only achieve financial freedom but also future-proof your approach to money management.

In the pages that follow, we'll explore everything from the basics of setting up a budget to the intricacies of AI-driven investment portfolios.

Your journey starts with a single step, and every chapter is a stride forward.

You'll learn how to leverage multiple income streams, reduce and manage debt, and prepare for the unexpected with an emergency fund. Each chapter will provide practical, step-by-step guidance, as well as motivational insights to keep you inspired and focused.

Financial independence isn't a finish line; it's a mindset and a series of smart choices.

The journey to financial independence isn't a race—it's a series of intentional steps. Some days you'll make great progress; other days, setbacks may occur. But with AI as your ally and the right strategies in place, you'll find yourself moving steadily closer to the life you envision. So, get ready to take control of your financial future, embrace the potential of AI, and start building a life defined by freedom, security, and opportunity.

Chapter – 2:
Understanding Financial Independence in the Modern World

Financial independence isn't a dream; it's a decision.

For many people, financial independence seems like a far-off goal, something achievable only by the wealthy or ultra-disciplined. However, financial independence isn't an exclusive club—it's an approach to money and lifestyle that anyone can adopt with the right mindset and strategies. At its core, financial independence is about freedom: the freedom to live on your terms, make choices that align with your values, and not be shackled to a nine-to-five job unless you want to be. This chapter will unpack what financial independence really means and why it's more attainable today than ever before.

Financial independence is a custom-made suit, not one-size-fits-all.

Each person's vision of financial independence is unique, shaped by their individual values, goals, and lifestyles. For some, it means the ability to retire early and travel the world; for others, it could be the peace of mind that comes from knowing they're financially secure enough to start a passion project. Your personal definition of financial independence will drive your journey, and it's essential to clarify what it means to you.

Defining Financial Independence

Financial independence, in its simplest form, means having enough income to cover your living expenses without actively working for money.

When your money works harder than you do, you're on the right path.

This can be achieved through various sources of income—investments, rental properties, businesses, and other passive income streams. The idea is that these income sources generate enough cash flow to cover your essential expenses, so you can focus on what truly matters to you, whether that's spending time with family, pursuing hobbies, or working on projects that don't necessarily generate income.

Imagine waking up on a Monday morning and knowing that you're working by choice, not by necessity.

Financial independence is the freedom to work for passion, not for paychecks.

It's not just about escaping the workforce; it's about escaping financial stress. This freedom allows you to make decisions based on your values rather than your financial situation.

The Financial Independence Formula: Income > Expenses

The fundamental principle behind financial independence is simple:

Spend less than you earn, and invest the difference.

While it sounds easy, putting it into practice requires discipline and, often, a shift in mindset. Financial independence doesn't happen overnight. It's the result of consistent, intentional actions, small choices that, over time, accumulate into substantial progress.

For many, this journey begins with controlling expenses and increasing savings. But remember, it's not only about frugality; it's about creating value. Increasing your income, whether through side hustles, skill development, or investments, accelerates your journey. Cut costs where it matters; invest where it counts. Every dollar you save or earn gets you one step closer to the freedom you're seeking.

Why Financial Independence Matters Today

The future belongs to the financially independent. In today's uncertain economy, financial independence offers a security net and a pathway to resilience. Jobs are no longer as secure as they once were, industries change, and even our careers can pivot at any time. Financial independence is like a safety buffer; it ensures that if life throws you a curveball, your finances aren't an added source of stress.

Beyond security, financial independence allows you to focus on what's truly fulfilling. Many people feel trapped in jobs that don't align with their passions or values simply because they need the paycheck. With financial independence, you gain the freedom to make choices that align with your purpose rather than just financial need.

When money is not your master, purpose becomes your guide.

Building a Vision for Your Financial Independence

Before diving into strategies and numbers, take a moment to define what financial independence means to you. This personal vision will keep you motivated and focused as you progress. Ask yourself questions like:

- What does financial independence look like for me?

- How much money do I need to live comfortably without working?

- What are my values, and how does financial freedom support them?

Your vision of independence is your compass—set it, and let it guide you.

Write down your vision and keep it visible, whether on a sticky note, a vision board, or as a reminder on your phone. This visual cue will help you stay aligned with your goals, especially when the journey feels challenging.

The Emotional Side of Financial Independence

Financial independence isn't just numbers; it's a mindset.

Often, we think of financial goals as purely practical, but they are deeply emotional as well. Reaching for financial independence involves breaking away from social expectations, challenging habits, and developing resilience. It requires us to confront fears about money, scarcity, and self-worth.

Money has an emotional weight; for some, it represents security, for others, status, and for many, it signifies freedom. Understanding your relationship with money and examining any limiting beliefs can be a powerful step toward achieving financial independence.

Change your money mindset, and you'll change your financial destiny.

When you see money as a tool to build freedom rather than as a source of stress, the journey to financial independence becomes less about sacrifice and more about empowerment.

Steps to Start Your Financial Independence Journey

"Every journey begins with a single step—and financial independence is no different."

With a clear vision in place, it's time to move from ideas to actions. Many people feel paralyzed at the start, unsure of where to begin, but the truth is that small, consistent steps are the key to achieving your goals. Here are some foundational steps to get you started on your path to financial independence.

1. Assess Your Current Financial Situation

You can't improve what you don't understand.

Start by taking a realistic look at your current financial status. List your sources of income, track your expenses, and calculate your net worth (assets minus liabilities). This financial assessment serves as your baseline, giving you a clear picture of where you stand and identifying areas where you can improve.

Use budgeting apps or personal finance software to help track your expenses and categorize your spending habits. Many AI-driven tools can automate this process, providing insights that reveal where your money goes each month.

Financial clarity is the foundation of financial independence.

2. Set Clear, Measurable Goals

Once you know your starting point, define your financial goals. It's not enough to say, "I want to be financially independent." Break down this goal into specific, measurable steps, like saving a certain amount per month or reaching a particular investment target.

For example, you might set a short-term goal of saving $10,000 in an emergency fund and a long-term goal of achieving $1 million in investment assets by age 50.

When your goals are clear, your path becomes obvious.

These goals will serve as your roadmap, keeping you motivated and on track as you progress toward financial independence.

3. Embrace the Power of Budgeting

A budget isn't a constraint—it's a compass.

Many people view budgeting as restrictive, but in reality, it's a powerful tool that gives you control over your finances. A well-structured budget helps you allocate resources to the things that matter most while cutting back on unnecessary expenses. Remember, the goal isn't to eliminate all pleasure but to spend intentionally.

A practical budgeting method to consider is the 50/30/20 rule: allocate 50% of your income to essentials, 30% to discretionary spending, and 20% to savings and investments. This balanced approach allows for responsible spending without depriving yourself. And with AI-driven budgeting apps, you can track your spending effortlessly, receive reminders, and even get recommendations on where to cut back.

With the right budget, your money starts working for you

4. Start Investing Early and Consistently

The earlier you start, the faster your money grows.

Investing is one of the most powerful tools for achieving financial independence. By investing wisely, you allow your money to grow through compounding, which can significantly increase your wealth over time. Even small amounts invested consistently can lead to substantial growth in the long run.

Explore low-cost, diversified investment options like index funds, exchange-traded funds (ETFs), and retirement accounts. With the help of AI tools, you can simplify the investment process, receiving personalized portfolio recommendations and tracking your investment performance.

Investing is planting seeds for a future where money isn't a worry.

5. Build Multiple Income Streams

One income stream is vulnerable; multiple income streams are powerful.

Relying on a single source of income can be risky, especially in today's unpredictable job market. Building multiple income streams not only increases your earning potential but also adds financial security.

Explore options like freelance work, side businesses, or even passive income from rental properties, dividends, or royalties. AI can assist here too—many platforms offer data-driven insights into freelance demand, real estate trends, and even profitable side hustle ideas.

Every new income stream is a step closer to freedom.

6. Manage Debt Strategically

Debt is one of the biggest barriers to financial independence.

Debt is a weight; financial independence is freedom.

If you're carrying debt, especially high-interest debt like credit card balances, make a plan to pay it off as quickly as possible. The avalanche method (paying off debts with the highest interest first) and the snowball method (starting with the smallest balances) are both effective strategies.

Using AI-powered financial tools, you can automate debt repayment plans, track interest rates, and visualize your debt payoff timeline. Each payment brings you closer to your goal of financial independence.

Every dollar directed at debt is a dollar invested in your future.

7. Build an Emergency Fund

An emergency fund is a financial safety net, covering unexpected expenses like medical bills, car repairs, or job loss.

An emergency fund isn't optional; it's essential.

Aim to save at least three to six months' worth of living expenses in a separate, easily accessible account. This fund will prevent you from dipping into your investments or going into debt when surprises arise.

AI-based savings apps can help automate this process, rounding up purchases and transferring small amounts to your emergency fund. These incremental contributions add up over time, helping you build a robust safety net with minimal effort.

An emergency fund isn't just money; it's peace of mind.

The Mindset Shift: Building Wealth for Freedom, Not Just Riches

Wealth is measured by freedom, not figures.

Financial independence isn't about becoming wealthy for wealth's sake; it's about creating a life where money is a tool, not a constraint. It's about building a sustainable lifestyle that gives you the freedom to pursue your passions, make choices without financial pressure, and live on your terms.

To achieve financial independence, cultivate a mindset that values intentionality, discipline, and long-term vision. This means prioritizing your goals over immediate gratification, embracing learning as a lifelong journey, and viewing every step you take as an investment in your future.

Your mindset is your greatest asset on the road to independence.

In the coming chapters, we'll dive deeper into each of these strategies, providing you with practical tools, tips, and insights to bring your vision of financial independence to life. You'll discover that this journey isn't about perfection—it's about progress, resilience, and the choices you make daily. With AI as your ally and a clear roadmap, financial independence is within reach.

Chapter – 3:
The Role of AI in Financial Management

AI is the bridge between your finances today and the financial freedom you seek tomorrow.

The concept of Artificial Intelligence (AI) has moved from science fiction into our everyday lives, influencing everything from our online shopping recommendations to voice-activated assistants in our homes. But AI is more than a convenience tool—it's a game-changer in personal finance, offering the average person access to insights and strategies once reserved for financial experts.

AI's potential in financial management lies in its ability to process vast amounts of data quickly, spot patterns, and make personalized recommendations. In finance, where every decision can impact your future, having a tool that provides real-time, data-driven insights is invaluable.

With AI, your financial decisions are no longer guesses; they're informed choices.

This chapter delves into how AI is revolutionizing personal finance, exploring specific tools and strategies that can help you reach financial independence more efficiently.

The Power of AI: Why Now?

In the past, building wealth and managing finances required either an extensive knowledge of finance or expensive advisors. But now, AI has made financial planning, investing, and budgeting accessible to everyone.

AI democratizes wealth-building—everyone can have access to expert financial guidance.

By analyzing data from millions of users, market trends, and personal behaviors, AI tools can provide insights tailored to your individual goals, lifestyle, and financial status.

Imagine trying to track every cent, monitor every market fluctuation, or assess every possible investment on your own—it's virtually impossible. AI simplifies this by performing these complex tasks instantaneously, freeing you from the stress and letting you focus on decision-making.

AI handles the details, so you can handle the big picture.

AI-Driven Budgeting and Expense Tracking

One of the most accessible uses of AI in finance is budgeting and expense tracking.

Budgeting isn't about restriction—it's about intention.

AI-powered budgeting apps, such as Mint, YNAB (You Need A Budget), and PocketGuard, have redefined how people manage their money. These tools automatically categorize your expenses, alert you to unusual spending, and even recommend adjustments based on your financial goals.

For example, if your goal is to save for a down payment on a house, AI-driven budgeting tools can identify where to cut unnecessary spending, suggest optimal saving amounts, and even alert you when you're veering off track. Many of these apps also feature automation, like setting aside a portion of your paycheck as savings or paying bills on time, so you don't have to worry about missing crucial payments.

With AI, budgeting isn't just a monthly task; it's a seamless part of your lifestyle.

Expense tracking goes hand-in-hand with budgeting. AI tools analyze your spending habits over time and provide insights on how to better allocate your resources. They can even send you alerts on recurring expenses, like subscriptions you may have forgotten. By knowing exactly where your money is going each month, you're empowered to make smarter financial decisions.

Awareness is the first step to control, and AI gives you that awareness on a silver platter.

Personalized Investment Strategies

Investing can be intimidating, especially if you're new to it.

You don't need to be an expert to invest wisely; you just need the right tools.

AI has made it easier than ever for beginners to enter the world of investing, with robo-advisors like Betterment, Wealthfront, and Acorns leading the way. These platforms use AI algorithms to analyze your risk tolerance, investment goals, and time horizon, then create a diversified portfolio tailored specifically to you.

Robo-advisors make investing accessible, managing everything from portfolio rebalancing to tax-loss harvesting. For those unfamiliar with investing, this means that your portfolio is continuously optimized to yield the best possible returns based on your goals.

With robo-advisors, you're not just investing; you're investing smartly.

AI also helps seasoned investors make more informed decisions. Advanced AI platforms like Kensho and Alpaca provide data-driven insights into market trends, enabling users to identify investment opportunities and risks faster than ever before. These platforms can analyze countless factors—economic indicators, news sentiment, and even social media trends—to help investors stay ahead.

For those looking to actively trade, AI-powered stock-picking apps like Zignaly or Tickeron offer suggestions based on sophisticated predictive algorithms. However, it's worth noting that while AI can offer insights, active investing still carries risk, and no algorithm can guarantee returns.

AI empowers, but the final decision—and responsibility—always rests with you.

Debt Management and Optimization with AI

Debt doesn't have to be a roadblock; with AI, it becomes a roadmap.

Many people struggle with managing debt, whether it's student loans, credit card debt, or mortgages. AI tools have made debt management easier by offering tailored strategies to help users pay off debt faster.

Apps like Tally and Credit Karma use AI algorithms to analyze your debts, interest rates, and repayment schedules, suggesting the most effective payoff strategies for your unique situation.

For example, Tally consolidates credit card debt and then creates a custom repayment plan to help you save on interest. Credit Karma, on the other hand, provides recommendations based on your credit score and financial profile, alerting you to potential savings opportunities and personalized loan options.

AI doesn't just help you pay down debt—it helps you optimize your finances.

AI can also be instrumental in improving your credit score. By analyzing your credit history, spending habits, and debt levels, AI tools can identify behaviors that may be negatively impacting your score and provide actionable steps to improve it. They can even set up payment reminders to ensure you're never late, which is crucial for maintaining or boosting credit health.

AI for Savings and Emergency Funds

Saving money is easier when you automate it.

Setting aside money for future goals or emergencies is essential for financial health, but it can be challenging to stay consistent. AI can help automate and accelerate your savings, turning it into a habit rather than a chore. Apps like Digit and Qapital use AI to analyze your spending habits and transfer small, manageable amounts into savings on your behalf.

Digit, for example, automatically moves small amounts from your checking account to savings based on your cash flow, so you save without even realizing it. Qapital allows you to set up "rules" for saving, such as saving $5 every time you make a purchase or rounding up transactions to the nearest dollar, with the difference going straight into savings.

AI helps you save painlessly, making sure that your goals are never left unfunded.

For building an emergency fund, these AI tools can be especially useful, helping you set aside a financial buffer without straining your monthly budget. Over time, these small, automatic transfers accumulate into a safety net, ready to cover unexpected expenses. This sense of preparedness contributes not only to financial stability but also to peace of mind.

With AI, saving becomes second nature—one less thing to worry about.

AI in Retirement Planning

Retirement isn't an age; it's a financial milestone.

Planning for retirement can seem like a complex and distant goal, especially for younger individuals. However, it's crucial to begin early, and with AI, retirement planning has become far more accessible and straightforward. Traditional retirement planning often involves consulting financial advisors to assess income needs, estimate costs, and select investments, but AI has streamlined much of this process.

AI-powered retirement planning tools, like Bloom and Fidelity's retirement calculators, assess your current savings, anticipated retirement age, and spending needs to generate a personalized retirement strategy. These tools can calculate how much you need to save each month, which types of accounts to contribute to, and which investment allocations are optimal for your specific goals.

AI helps you retire smarter by crafting a plan that grows with you.

For instance, Blooom connects to your 401(k) account, analyzes your investment choices, and provides recommendations on how to optimize your portfolio for growth or adjust it as retirement nears. The platform even considers factors like market volatility and inflation, ensuring that your retirement strategy is both resilient and adaptable. With AI, you can actively track your progress and make adjustments as needed, knowing that you're moving closer to financial independence each day.

Risk Management and Financial Security

Risk is inevitable; managing it is essential.

Whether it's market fluctuations, inflation, or unexpected expenses, every financial plan faces risk. One of the most powerful applications of AI in finance is its ability to analyze and mitigate these risks. AI algorithms constantly analyze massive datasets, identifying trends and warning users about potential financial risks well in advance.

For investors, platforms like ZestFinance and Kensho use AI to analyze economic data, company performance, and even social media sentiment, alerting you to risks that might affect your portfolio. This proactive approach helps protect your investments from unforeseen changes and enables you to make informed decisions during volatile market periods.

With AI, you're not just reacting to risk—you're preparing for it.

AI also aids in personal financial security. For example, fraud detection algorithms monitor your transactions in real-time, flagging any unusual activity to prevent identity theft or unauthorized charges. Many banks and financial apps incorporate AI-driven security features that learn from your behavior and notify you instantly if something seems suspicious.

Financial independence starts with financial security, and AI is your safeguard.

AI and Financial Literacy: Learning While You Grow

AI isn't just a tool—it's a teacher.

Financial literacy is one of the cornerstones of financial independence. AI-powered platforms have made learning about personal finance easier than ever. Apps like Cleo and Finimize provide users with bite-sized financial tips, explanations of complex concepts, and personalized advice based on individual financial situations.

For example, Cleo is a chatbot that not only helps you track spending and manage your budget but also answers questions about credit scores, interest rates, and financial planning. Its conversational interface makes finance less intimidating, helping you build knowledge and confidence. Finimize, on the other hand, offers daily insights on market trends, news, and investment strategies, making it easier to understand what's happening in the financial world.

With AI, every financial decision becomes a learning opportunity.

By using these AI tools, you don't just manage your money—you learn the 'why' and 'how' behind each decision. This knowledge equips you to make smarter choices in the future, empowering you with financial independence that's based on understanding rather than guesswork.

The Ethical Side of AI in Finance

Power comes with responsibility, even in personal finance.

While AI offers remarkable benefits, it's essential to be mindful of the ethical implications surrounding its use. Privacy concerns are significant, as financial apps often require access to sensitive data. Make sure to review the data privacy policies of any platform you use, ensuring that your information is handled securely and responsibly.

Additionally, it's essential to remember that while AI can enhance your financial management, it shouldn't replace critical thinking. Algorithms can provide suggestions, but they lack the nuanced understanding of personal values, goals, and life circumstances that a human advisor might consider.

AI assists; you decide.

The best approach is to use AI as a supplement to, rather than a replacement for, your own judgment and financial knowledge.

Embracing AI: How to Get Started

The best time to start was yesterday; the next best time is now.

Embracing AI in your financial journey doesn't require a tech background or extensive experience. Start small by exploring a few highly-rated AI-driven tools in budgeting, saving, and investing. Choose platforms that align with your immediate needs and goals, allowing you to gradually integrate more complex tools as you gain confidence.

1. **Identify Your Goals**: Are you looking to save more, pay down debt, or invest? Start with one primary goal and choose AI tools that cater to it.

2. **Explore Budgeting Apps**: Download an AI-powered budgeting app like Mint or PocketGuard to gain visibility into your spending and saving habits.

3. **Try a Robo-Advisor**: If you're new to investing, open an account with a robo-advisor such as Betterment or Wealthfront. These platforms make it easy to invest with as little as $10 and offer guidance on portfolio growth.

4. **Set Up an Emergency Fund**: Use apps like Digit or Qapital to automate your savings for a financial cushion. These AI tools assess your cash flow and help you build an emergency fund without much thought.

5. **Learn Along the Way**: Follow platforms like Finimize or Cleo for financial literacy tips, market updates, and personal finance guidance.

The more you know, the more you grow.

The Future of AI in Personal Finance

The future of finance is here, and it's only getting smarter.

The role of AI in personal finance is still evolving. Emerging AI technologies are expected to enhance financial management further, potentially even integrating blockchain and cryptocurrency capabilities. For those invested in financial independence, staying informed on these developments can open new opportunities.

The ongoing improvements in machine learning mean that AI will continue to become more intuitive, providing increasingly sophisticated insights and potentially even predicting long-term financial patterns. Imagine having an AI that can project your financial future with remarkable accuracy or one that adjusts your financial plan automatically based on changing economic conditions.

With AI, the possibilities are endless, but the journey starts today.

Wrapping Up: AI as Your Financial Ally

Embracing AI in personal finance isn't about relinquishing control; it's about enhancing it.

You're the driver; AI is the navigator.

These tools offer data-driven insights, personalized recommendations, and effortless automation, all designed to help you make more informed decisions on your path to financial independence.

As you move forward, remember that AI is just one tool in your financial toolkit. It can help you maximize your resources, streamline your budgeting, optimize investments, and build a robust financial foundation. But ultimately, financial independence is a journey shaped by your goals, values, and actions.

AI gives you the tools, but the decisions—and the rewards—are yours.

With a commitment to learning, an openness to innovation, and a focus on your long-term goals, you can harness the power of AI to create a financial future where freedom and opportunity are within reach. The road to financial independence has never been more accessible, and with AI as your ally, there's no limit to where it can take you.

Chapter – 4:
Setting the Foundation – Assessing Your Current Financial Situation

Financial independence begins with knowing where you stand.

Before you can map out your path to financial freedom, it's essential to take a close look at your current financial situation. Think of it as drawing the first map for a long journey—without knowing your starting point, it's impossible to navigate effectively. Many people avoid assessing their finances out of fear, but gaining clarity on your income, expenses, assets, and liabilities is the first step toward control and confidence.

Facing your finances head-on is the most powerful move you can make.

The goal of this chapter is to guide you through an in-depth assessment of your financial situation. With an honest view of your finances, you'll understand your current strengths and areas for improvement, setting a solid foundation to achieve your long-term goals.

Income: Knowing What Comes In

Start with your income, as it's the primary driver of your financial situation. Income includes not only your paycheck from a job but also any additional sources like freelance work, rental properties, or dividends from investments. Listing all your income sources helps you see exactly what's available to you each month.

If your income varies, such as with freelance work, calculate an average based on the last six to twelve months. This will give you a realistic picture of your monthly resources, allowing you to plan effectively.

Income is the engine of financial independence—know its power and its limits.

Expenses: Understanding Where the Money Goes

Expenses are often the trickiest part of a financial assessment, but they're also the most revealing. Knowing where your money goes each month helps you understand your spending habits and identify areas for potential savings. Begin by categorizing your expenses:

1. **Fixed Expenses** – These are regular costs that remain relatively stable each month, like rent, mortgage payments, insurance, and loan repayments. Fixed expenses are often non-negotiable, so they form the foundation of your budget.

2. **Variable Expenses** – These fluctuate monthly and include items like groceries, utilities, entertainment, and transportation. Variable expenses offer more flexibility, making them a target for potential savings.

3. **Discretionary Spending** – This category covers non-essential expenses such as dining out, subscriptions, hobbies, and entertainment. While discretionary spending adds enjoyment to life, keeping it in check is essential for achieving financial goals.

Tracking expenses can be made easier with AI-powered budgeting tools. Apps like Mint, YNAB, or PocketGuard automatically categorize your transactions, providing a detailed breakdown of where your money goes.

Know your expenses—where the money flows, control grows.

Assets: Calculating What You Own

Assets are the building blocks of wealth. They represent the resources you have that can contribute to financial independence. Assets can include cash, savings accounts, investments, real estate, retirement accounts, and even valuable personal possessions like a car or jewelry.

When assessing assets, consider both liquid assets (cash or easily converted to cash) and non-liquid assets (such as real estate or retirement accounts that are not easily accessible). List these assets with their current market value, but keep in mind that their value may fluctuate. For example, investments in stocks or mutual funds will change with the market.

Assets are the seeds of wealth; plant them wisely.

The goal is to maximize assets over time through consistent saving and investing. Having a clear list of your assets also shows where you have room to grow. For example, if your emergency fund is smaller than you'd like, focus on building it up over time.

Liabilities: Calculating What You Owe

Liabilities are the flip side of assets—they represent your financial obligations. This includes all outstanding debts such as mortgages, student loans, car loans, credit card balances, and any other personal loans. List each debt, its outstanding balance, the interest rate, and the minimum monthly payment. Knowing the interest rate on each debt can help you prioritize repayment effectively, focusing first on high-interest debts like credit cards.

Liabilities are weights; shedding them lightens your financial load.

Debt can feel overwhelming, but assessing it accurately provides perspective. Many people find that understanding their debt in detail makes it more manageable and even motivates them to pay it down faster. The goal is to reduce liabilities over time, as this will free up your resources for saving and investing.

Calculating Your Net Worth: The True Financial Snapshot

Once you've listed all income, expenses, assets, and liabilities, it's time to calculate your net worth. Net worth is a powerful indicator of financial health and is calculated by subtracting your liabilities from your assets.

Net worth isn't just a number—it's your financial scorecard.

A positive net worth means you own more than you owe, while a negative net worth indicates debt exceeds assets. Don't be discouraged if your net worth is lower than expected or even negative; this assessment is the starting point, not the final destination.

Tracking your net worth over time, either monthly or quarterly, can help you see the impact of your financial decisions. Many budgeting and finance apps automatically track net worth, giving you a real-time snapshot of your progress toward financial independence.

Evaluating Cash Flow: The Heartbeat of Financial Health

In addition to net worth, understanding your cash flow—how money moves in and out of your finances—is crucial. Cash flow gives you insight into how well you're managing your money month to month. Ideally, you want positive cash flow, where income exceeds expenses, as this surplus can be directed toward savings, investments, or debt repayment.

Calculate your monthly cash flow by subtracting your total monthly expenses from your total monthly income.

Cash flow is the lifeblood of your finances; keep it positive to thrive.

If you're experiencing negative cash flow, consider adjusting expenses or exploring ways to increase income. Even small changes, like cutting down discretionary spending or starting a side hustle, can have a big impact over time. Positive cash flow is the first step toward building wealth and achieving financial independence.

Creating a Financial Snapshot

With a full picture of your finances, you can create a "financial snapshot" that consolidates all key information: income, expenses, assets, liabilities, net worth, and cash flow. This snapshot gives you a clear understanding of where you stand financially and serves as a baseline to track your progress.

A financial snapshot is your compass—use it to chart the course ahead.

A financial snapshot also reveals areas for improvement, whether it's paying down debt, building assets, or adjusting spending habits.

Reviewing this snapshot monthly or quarterly can help you stay accountable, adjust goals, and ensure you're on track to financial independence.

Chapter – 5:
The Power of Budgeting and Automation

Budgeting is the backbone of financial independence.

For many people, budgeting feels restrictive, a chore they avoid or only attempt sporadically. Yet, when used correctly, a budget is one of the most powerful tools on your path to financial freedom. Rather than seeing it as a limitation, think of budgeting as a way to take control of your finances. It provides the clarity and discipline needed to allocate resources effectively, make informed financial decisions, and ensure your spending aligns with your long-term goals.

When you know where your money goes, you can decide where it should go.

The purpose of budgeting is simple: it helps you spend intentionally. By creating a budget, you set a clear outline of your income, expenses, and savings. This outline serves as a financial roadmap, guiding every dollar toward its best use, whether that's covering essential expenses, reducing debt, or building your investment portfolio. In this chapter, we'll dive into how to create a budget that works, explore different budgeting methods, and explain how to leverage automation for greater efficiency and success.

The Benefits of Budgeting for Financial Independence

Budgeting turns dreams into actionable goals.

At its core, budgeting is about empowering yourself to achieve financial freedom. When you have a budget, you have a concrete plan that bridges your current situation and future aspirations. Each month, it shows you where you stand financially, helping you understand if you're moving closer to or further from your goals.

Some of the key benefits of budgeting include:

1. **Improved Financial Awareness** – A budget brings your income, expenses, and savings goals into sharp focus, making it easier to make informed decisions.

2. **Reduced Stress** – With a clear plan for your finances, unexpected expenses become less overwhelming, as you'll have contingencies in place.

3. **Enhanced Savings and Investment Opportunities** – A budget helps you identify surplus funds that can be directed toward savings, investments, or debt repayment.

4. **Motivation and Accountability** – Tracking your progress in real-time allows you to celebrate small wins and adjust if you deviate from the plan.

Budgeting isn't just about saving money; it's about aligning your spending with your values and priorities. This alignment gives every dollar a purpose and ensures that your financial choices support the life you want to create.

Setting Up Your Budget: The Basics

Every budget starts with a vision.

Creating a budget begins with an honest assessment of your income and expenses. Start by gathering all necessary financial information, including paychecks, bills, statements, and receipts. Break down your budget into essential components to get a clear picture of where your money is coming from and where it's going.

1. **Income**: List all sources of income, including your salary, freelance work, investments, or any other revenue streams. If your income fluctuates, calculate an average over a few months to get a reliable figure.

2. **Fixed Expenses**: These are recurring, often non-negotiable costs such as rent, mortgage payments, insurance premiums, loan payments, and utility bills. Fixed expenses are stable each month, forming the foundation of your spending plan.

3. **Variable Expenses**: These costs can change month to month and include items like groceries, entertainment, dining out, transportation, and discretionary purchases. This category provides more flexibility for adjustments.

4. **Savings and Investments**: Allocate a portion of your income to savings and investments. This could include emergency fund contributions, retirement accounts, or other investment vehicles that support long-term goals.

5. **Debt Repayment**: If you have outstanding debts, make them part of your budget. Knowing how much you allocate toward debt each month helps you track progress and adjust as needed.

With these categories defined, you have a roadmap to financial clarity.

Budgeting Methods: Finding What Works for You

There's no one-size-fits-all budget—choose a method that suits your style.

Different people have different spending habits, financial goals, and preferences. The best budgeting method is one that you can stick to consistently. Here are three popular approaches to consider:

1. The 50/30/20 Budget

This method divides your income into three main categories:

- **50% for Essentials**: Basic needs like housing, utilities, groceries, and transportation.

- **30% for Discretionary Spending**: Fun and personal enjoyment, like dining out, hobbies, and non-essential shopping.

- **20% for Savings and Debt Repayment**: Funds allocated for future needs, including investments, savings accounts, and paying down debt.

The 50/30/20 budget is straightforward and flexible, making it a good choice for beginners. It provides structure while allowing room for discretionary spending without guilt.

2. The Zero-Based Budget

In a zero-based budget, every dollar is assigned a specific purpose, from income to expenses to savings, so that income minus expenses equals zero. This method forces you to account for each dollar, ensuring that none is left idle or unplanned.

A zero-based budget can be particularly effective for those who want tight control over their finances, as it leaves little room for unintentional spending. It's ideal for maximizing savings or aggressively paying down debt.

3. The Envelope System

The envelope system is a cash-based approach where you allocate physical cash into envelopes labeled for each spending category, like groceries, dining out, or entertainment. When the money in an envelope is gone, spending for that category stops until the next month.

This method is helpful for anyone looking to curb overspending, especially in discretionary categories. While it may feel outdated in today's digital world, many budgeting apps offer a digital version of the envelope system, allowing you to track spending in specific categories without physical cash.

The best budget is one that fits your life and helps you achieve your goals.

Automating Your Budget: Letting Technology Do the Work

Automation brings consistency and ease to budgeting.

One of the biggest hurdles in budgeting is sticking to it month after month. Automating parts of your budget simplifies the process and ensures consistency. With automation, you don't have to rely solely on willpower or memory to maintain your budget. Instead, scheduled transfers, payments, and savings contributions happen automatically, making budgeting a seamless part of your routine.

Here's how to automate various components of your budget:

1. **Direct Deposit for Savings**: Arrange for a portion of your paycheck to go directly into a savings or investment account. This "pay yourself first" strategy prioritizes your savings goals without the temptation to spend the money first.

2. **Automated Bill Payments**: Set up automatic payments for fixed expenses like rent, utilities, and loan payments. This ensures timely payments, helping you avoid late fees and maintain good credit.

3. **Automatic Transfers to Debt Repayment**: If you're focused on paying down debt, set up an automatic monthly transfer to your debt account. This helps you stay on track without having to manually initiate payments.

4. **Recurring Investments**: Use investment platforms that support automated contributions. Many robo-advisors, like Betterment or Wealthfront, allow you to set up recurring deposits into your investment portfolio, helping you build wealth passively.

With automation, your budget works for you—even when you're not thinking about it.

Automation not only removes the mental burden of managing a budget but also fosters consistency, making it easier to achieve financial goals over time. In the next section, we'll discuss using AI-driven apps and tools to further enhance and simplify the budgeting process, setting you up for success without the hassle.

Using AI-Driven Tools to Enhance Budgeting

Let AI be your financial coach.

AI-driven tools have transformed budgeting, making it easier to manage finances in real-time and optimize spending habits. With features like automated tracking, personalized insights, and predictive analysis, AI tools allow you to make data-driven decisions, even if you're just beginning your financial journey. These tools continuously analyze your spending habits, alert you to trends, and recommend adjustments tailored to your goals.

Some popular AI-powered budgeting apps include:

- **Mint**: Tracks spending, categorizes expenses, and provides a comprehensive overview of your financial health.

- **YNAB (You Need A Budget)**: Focuses on the zero-based budgeting approach, helping users assign every dollar a purpose.

- **PocketGuard**: Shows exactly how much disposable income you have after accounting for bills, savings, and essentials.

These apps don't just track expenses; they actively provide insights that help you improve your budgeting strategy. Mint, for instance, might alert you to an increase in your dining-out expenses, prompting you to adjust and stay aligned with your budget goals. YNAB takes a proactive approach, reminding you to "roll with the punches" when unexpected expenses arise.

With AI tools, you have real-time insights that turn budgeting into a living, adaptable plan.

Advanced Automation Techniques for Budgeting

Turn budgeting into a set-and-forget system.

Beyond basic automation, advanced techniques allow you to take a more hands-off approach to budgeting. These strategies involve leveraging technology to handle multiple financial tasks automatically, reducing the amount of time and energy you spend managing money. Here's how to apply these advanced methods:

1. **Automatic Budget Adjustments**: Some AI-powered apps, like Digit, use machine learning to analyze your cash flow and adjust transfers to savings based on your spending habits. This adaptive approach ensures you save consistently without feeling restricted.

2. **Dynamic Spending Alerts**: Many budgeting apps now offer alerts that notify you when you're close to exceeding a set category limit. For instance, if your goal is to spend only $200 on dining out each month, an alert will let you know when you're nearing that threshold. This feature acts as a guardrail, keeping you from overspending.

3. **Recurring Expense Management**: Managing subscriptions and recurring expenses is often overlooked but can add up over time. Apps like Truebill and Trim automatically detect and track subscriptions, allowing you to cancel unnecessary services with a few clicks.

4. **Goal-Based Savings Plans**: Apps like Qapital allow users to create specific "goals" with individual savings rules. For example, you could set a rule to save $5 every time you make a purchase, which is then allocated to a vacation or emergency fund. This gamifies saving, making it more engaging and less of a chore.

Advanced automation transforms budgeting from a monthly task into a lifestyle.

Managing Variable Income with Budgeting and Automation

Budgeting for variable income requires flexibility and foresight.

If you have a variable income, such as freelance work or commissions, budgeting can feel challenging. With fluctuating earnings, it's essential to build flexibility into your budget. One effective method is to base your budget on a conservative estimate of your income, using the average of the last six to twelve months. By budgeting on the lower end, you create a cushion for months when income falls short.

In high-earning months, consider allocating extra funds to your savings or a buffer account. This surplus can be used during leaner months, helping to smooth out cash flow. Automating transfers to savings or an emergency fund during peak months can be particularly effective, ensuring that a portion of your income is consistently set aside.

By planning for fluctuations, variable income doesn't have to disrupt your path to financial independence.

The Power of Accountability in Budgeting

Accountability turns budgeting from theory into practice.

Staying accountable to your budget is key to making it work in the long term. Regularly reviewing your budget and progress helps keep you on track and identify any patterns in your spending habits. Consider these accountability strategies:

1. **Weekly or Monthly Check-Ins**: Set aside time each week or month to review your budget, tracking your expenses, and adjusting your allocations as needed. This routine ensures that you're aware of your spending in real time and can make timely adjustments.

2. **Partner with a Budget Buddy**: For added accountability, pair up with a friend or partner who shares similar financial goals. Checking in with each other regularly keeps you both motivated and provides an opportunity to exchange budgeting tips and insights.

3. **Use Visualization Tools**: Many budgeting apps provide charts and visual summaries that make it easy to see where your money is going. Visual aids can help you understand your progress at a glance and reinforce positive habits.

Accountability keeps your budget dynamic, helping you adapt to changes and stay committed to your goals. Over time, sticking to a budget becomes second nature, simplifying your path to financial independence.

Maximizing Savings with Automated Budgeting

Automation makes saving seamless.

One of the most effective ways to maximize savings is by automating contributions to dedicated accounts. By setting up automated transfers, you ensure that a portion of your income is consistently directed toward savings goals. This "pay yourself first" strategy removes the temptation to spend money before it's saved.

Consider creating separate savings accounts for specific goals, such as an emergency fund, a vacation fund, or a down payment fund. Most banks allow you to set up multiple savings accounts, making it easy to designate each one for a specific purpose. Automating transfers into these accounts aligns with your budget, helping you reach your goals faster.

For those who want to boost their savings even further, round-up savings features are another useful tool. Many banks and budgeting apps offer this feature, which rounds up each purchase to the nearest dollar and transfers the difference into savings. For instance, if you spend $3.75 on coffee, $0.25 will be automatically saved. While small, these incremental amounts add up over time, making saving painless.

Automated savings means every dollar has a purpose, bringing you closer to financial freedom.

Final Thoughts on Budgeting and Automation

Budgeting isn't about restriction; it's about intention.

Budgeting, when done thoughtfully, gives you the power to control your financial journey. By aligning your spending with your values and goals, you're building a roadmap to a life of financial independence. Automation amplifies this process, reducing the effort required to maintain a budget and consistently save toward your dreams.

Embracing budgeting and automation transforms your finances into a structured, manageable system that works with your life, not against it. With a clear budget in place and the support of AI-driven tools, every dollar you earn is a step closer to freedom.

Budgeting and automation are the keys to achieving financial independence—unlock the door and step through.

As you continue on your journey, remember that budgeting isn't a one-time activity. It's an evolving tool that grows with you, adjusting to changes in income, lifestyle, and priorities. By consistently investing in your budget, you're investing in yourself and your future. In the next chapter, we'll explore taking actionable steps toward financial independence by setting realistic goals, creating achievable milestones, and building a lifestyle that supports your vision of financial freedom.

Your budget is the blueprint to a life of choice and freedom—use it wisely.

Chapter – 6:
Taking Action: Small Steps Toward Big Goals (The Butterfly Effect)

Financial independence isn't a giant leap; it's a series of small steps.

When it comes to financial freedom, the journey can feel overwhelming if you try to tackle everything at once. Setting out with the ambition to eliminate all debt, build a substantial emergency fund, and invest for the future can seem daunting. However, by breaking down these big goals into smaller, achievable actions, you transform the journey into a manageable and rewarding process.

This chapter emphasizes the importance of actionable steps and realistic milestones in reaching financial independence. Instead of getting lost in the big picture, we'll focus on strategies to gain momentum and stay motivated as you achieve one small goal at a time.

The Power of Starting Small

Big goals are made of small actions.

Starting small may seem counterintuitive when you have ambitious financial goals, but it's one of the most effective strategies for building lasting financial habits. Small, consistent actions create momentum, making each step easier and more sustainable. Rather than aiming to save a large amount all at once, start with a small monthly savings target. Over time, this habit becomes second nature, allowing you to gradually increase your savings.

For example, if you're new to budgeting, don't aim to overhaul all spending categories immediately. Start by tracking just one area, such as dining out. By focusing on a single category, you can build the discipline to monitor and adjust spending without feeling overwhelmed. Once you're comfortable, expand your budget to include other areas, eventually creating a comprehensive financial plan.

Small actions repeated consistently lead to big results.

Setting Realistic Milestones

Milestones turn a long journey into achievable phases.

Setting realistic milestones makes the path to financial independence more manageable and helps maintain motivation. Break down your primary goals—such as building an emergency fund, paying off debt, or saving for retirement—into smaller, time-bound targets. For example, instead of focusing on saving $10,000 for an emergency fund, set an initial milestone to save $1,000. Once you reach that goal, celebrate it, then set the next milestone.

Milestones also serve as checkpoints, allowing you to assess progress and make adjustments as needed. If you find yourself struggling to reach a milestone, analyze what's holding you back and consider adjusting your approach. Financial independence isn't a race; it's about steady, intentional progress.

Some examples of realistic milestones include:

- **Save $500 within the next two months** – Focused on building a small emergency buffer.

- **Pay off one high-interest credit card** – Reducing debt one account at a time.

- **Invest $100 monthly for six months** – Starting a routine of consistent contributions.

- **Reduce monthly dining expenses by 20%** – Small changes in discretionary spending.

By setting milestones, you create a roadmap for financial independence that feels achievable and motivating. Each milestone brings you closer to your long-term goals and reinforces your commitment to financial freedom.

Celebrate every milestone; each one is a step closer to your vision.

Building a Financial Routine

Consistency is the backbone of financial independence.

One of the most impactful ways to make progress is to develop a routine around your financial habits. A financial routine helps automate decision-making, reducing the mental load required to manage your finances. Just as you might have a morning routine to start the day, a financial routine establishes consistency in how you handle money.

Consider setting up regular "money dates" with yourself—time specifically set aside to review your budget, track your spending, and plan for the month ahead. These sessions don't need to be lengthy; even 30 minutes weekly can be enough to keep your financial goals on track.

An effective financial routine might include:

- **Weekly Spending Check-Ins**: Review your spending for the week, adjust any category if necessary, and identify areas for improvement.

- **Monthly Budget Review**: Adjust your budget to account for upcoming expenses, special events, or changes in income.

- **Quarterly Progress Reviews**: Evaluate your progress toward major financial goals, assess your net worth, and make adjustments to long-term plans.

Consistency is key—small actions become powerful habits over time.

Automating Progress with Technology

Automation simplifies progress and makes goals achievable.

The journey to financial independence is easier when certain actions become automatic. Automating savings, investments, and bill payments minimizes the need for constant oversight, helping you make progress even when life gets busy.

1. **Automate Savings Transfers**: Set up recurring transfers to your savings account immediately after your paycheck is deposited. This "pay yourself first" approach ensures that a portion of your income goes directly to savings, helping you build your emergency fund or reach other goals.

2. **Use Round-Up Features for Additional Savings**: Many banking apps and fintech platforms offer round-up features, where every purchase is rounded up to the nearest dollar, with the difference transferred to savings. These small amounts accumulate over time, adding up to a meaningful contribution without any extra effort.

3. **Schedule Investments**: Set up automated investments through a robo-advisor or investment platform, such as Betterment or Wealthfront. Scheduling regular deposits ensures consistent contributions, allowing you to benefit from dollar-cost averaging, where you invest a fixed amount regardless of market conditions.

4. **Automate Debt Payments**: If paying down debt is a priority, set up automatic payments for your minimum balances and schedule extra payments when possible. Automation ensures you stay consistent and reduce debt gradually, without missing any deadlines.

With automation, progress becomes effortless, and financial independence feels within reach.

Embracing the Concept of "Good Enough"

Progress doesn't require perfection.

One of the biggest obstacles to financial independence is the desire for perfection. Many people feel pressured to get every aspect of their finances "right" from the start, which can lead to frustration or even quitting when things don't go perfectly. Instead of aiming for perfection, embrace the concept of "good enough."

For example, if you can only save a small amount this month due to an unexpected expense, don't be discouraged. Making a consistent effort, even if it's not perfect, still brings you closer to your goals. Progress toward financial independence is about long-term persistence, not flawless execution.

Letting go of perfection also reduces stress, helping you stay motivated over time. Remember, the key to financial freedom is steady improvement, not perfection.

Good enough today is better than perfect tomorrow.

Staying Motivated with Small Wins

Small wins fuel big dreams.

Staying motivated is essential on the journey to financial independence, and nothing boosts motivation quite like celebrating small achievements. Each small win, whether it's sticking to your budget for a month or reaching a savings milestone, reinforces your commitment and builds momentum. Recognizing and rewarding your progress, no matter how minor it seems, can keep you inspired to reach the next milestone.

For example, if you hit a savings target, consider celebrating with a small treat or experience that doesn't break the budget—like a nice dinner at home or a day trip. This way, you associate your financial progress with a positive feeling. Some people create a "reward fund," setting aside a small amount specifically to celebrate milestones. This approach allows you to indulge occasionally without impacting your primary financial goals.

Every small win is a step closer to your dream life—enjoy the journey.

Visualizing Your Progress

Seeing your progress makes success feel tangible.

Visual aids can be powerful motivators. Tracking your progress visually—whether through charts, graphs, or even a simple progress bar—allows you to see how far you've come. Many budgeting apps offer visual summaries that make it easy to see monthly expenses, savings rates, and debt reduction. By watching your debt shrink or your savings grow, you get a clear, encouraging view of your journey.

Consider using a physical tracker if you prefer something tangible. For example, a debt payoff thermometer or savings goal chart allows you to color in sections as you progress. These visual reminders keep you engaged, helping you stay motivated and focused.

Make your progress visible—it's a powerful motivator.

Creating Habits That Support Your Goals

Habits are the foundation of financial freedom.

Creating good financial habits is essential for long-term success. Habits are actions we take automatically, so building ones that align with your financial goals ensures consistent progress. Developing habits like tracking your spending, reviewing your budget weekly, or transferring a set amount to savings each month simplifies the journey to financial independence.

Start by incorporating one habit at a time until it becomes routine. For instance, commit to checking your account balances every morning, or dedicate ten minutes every Friday to reviewing your weekly spending. As these actions become habitual, they reduce the mental effort needed to manage your finances, making it easier to stay on track without constant motivation.

Strong habits turn big goals into daily achievements.

Overcoming Obstacles and Staying Flexible

Obstacles are just opportunities for a new approach.

Life is unpredictable, and financial goals don't always go as planned. Unexpected expenses, changes in income, or personal challenges can disrupt progress. Instead of feeling discouraged, use these obstacles as opportunities to adjust your approach. Flexibility is key in achieving financial independence, and adapting your plans when needed helps you stay on course.

If an unexpected expense arises, you may need to temporarily reduce contributions to savings or debt repayment. Similarly, if you receive a bonus or windfall, consider using a portion to boost your progress. Adapting to changes ensures that you maintain forward momentum, even when life throws a curveball.

Flexibility is the secret weapon on the path to financial freedom.

Focusing on What You Can Control

Control what you can; adapt to what you can't.

Financial independence is a journey with ups and downs. While certain factors, like market fluctuations or unexpected expenses, are outside your control, focusing on what you can manage keeps you empowered. Your spending habits, savings rate, and debt repayment efforts are all within your influence, and these areas will have the most significant impact on your progress.

When external factors feel overwhelming, redirect your energy to the aspects you can control. For instance, if the market is volatile, focus on your budgeting and saving efforts rather than worrying about investment fluctuations. By keeping your focus on controllable actions, you reduce stress and maintain a sense of agency over your journey.

Financial freedom is built by controlling what you can and adapting to what you can't.

Tracking Your Net Worth to Measure Progress

Net worth is the ultimate scoreboard of financial independence.

One of the most effective ways to measure your progress toward financial independence is by tracking your net worth. Net worth, calculated by subtracting your liabilities from your assets, provides a clear snapshot of your financial health. As you pay down debt and grow your savings, your net worth will increase, serving as a powerful indicator of your progress.

Reviewing your net worth quarterly or even monthly helps you see the cumulative impact of your efforts. Watching your net worth grow can be incredibly motivating, reinforcing that every small step counts. Many budgeting apps automatically track net worth, making it easy to monitor without extra work.

Track your net worth regularly—it's a reflection of your hard work and dedication.

Using AI Tools to Stay on Course

AI keeps you on track, even when motivation wanes.

Leveraging AI tools in your financial routine can make it easier to stay consistent. Apps like Mint and YNAB provide personalized insights, automatically track spending, and help you stay within budget categories. They even alert you if you're veering off course, offering reminders to adjust as needed. By using these tools, you create a support system that helps maintain your progress, even during busy or challenging periods.

AI tools like Cleo and Digit can also gamify saving, offering motivational messages and tips to keep you engaged. These interactive features make it easier to stick with financial goals, reinforcing positive behavior through real-time feedback.

AI tools act as personal finance coaches, keeping you motivated every step of the way.

Building a "Financial Independence" Mindset

Financial independence starts in the mind.

Reaching financial independence requires more than just budgeting and saving; it requires a mindset shift. Building a mindset focused on long-term wealth and financial independence helps you view your decisions from a broader perspective. This mindset encourages delayed gratification, intentional spending, and consistent effort toward goals.

Instead of viewing budgeting as a restriction, see it as a tool that empowers you to prioritize what truly matters. Embrace the process, and remind yourself that each small decision contributes to the freedom you're building for your future self.

Cultivate a mindset that aligns with your financial goals—mindset drives action.

Final Thoughts on Taking Action

Action brings financial independence within reach.

The journey to financial independence doesn't require perfection; it requires action. By focusing on small, achievable steps, setting realistic milestones, and celebrating every win along the way, you're creating a roadmap that leads to freedom. Leveraging technology and building good habits simplify the process, allowing you to make progress without constant effort.

As you move forward, remember that financial independence is a long-term pursuit. Embrace the journey, adapt as needed, and maintain a focus on consistent action. Over time, the small steps you take today will add up to substantial progress, bringing you closer to a life defined by choice, freedom, and financial empowerment.

Each step forward is a commitment to your financial freedom—take that step with confidence.

Chapter – 7:
Investing with Confidence – AI and Wealth-Building

Investing isn't just for experts; it's for everyone willing to learn.

Investing is a powerful wealth-building tool that can fast-track your journey to financial independence. By putting your money to work through investments, you create an additional income stream that grows over time, amplifying your financial stability and freedom. Yet, many people feel intimidated by investing, assuming it's only for those with extensive knowledge or large sums of money. This misconception can prevent people from taking the first step toward financial growth.

The good news is that technology, especially AI, has made investing accessible and manageable for everyone, regardless of experience level. With AI-driven tools, you can create a diversified portfolio, manage risk, and optimize returns with minimal effort and oversight. This chapter will guide you through the basics of investing, show you how AI simplifies the process, and provide strategies to build a strong, future-focused investment portfolio.

Confidence in investing comes from understanding the basics and using the right tools.

Understanding the Basics of Investing

Every investor starts as a beginner.

Before diving into AI-driven tools and strategies, it's essential to understand some foundational concepts in investing. At its core, investing is the process of allocating money with the expectation of earning a return. Returns can come in different forms, such as stock dividends, interest payments, or capital gains from asset appreciation. Here are a few key terms to familiarize yourself with:

1. **Stocks** – Shares of a company that represent partial ownership. When you buy stocks, you own a piece of the company, and your investment value changes based on the company's performance and market conditions.

2. **Bonds** – Debt securities issued by corporations or governments. When you buy a bond, you're lending money to the issuer in exchange for periodic interest payments and the return of your principal at maturity.

3. **Mutual Funds** – Pooled investments managed by professionals. Mutual funds consist of various assets like stocks and bonds, offering instant diversification.

4. **Exchange-Traded Funds (ETFs)** – Similar to mutual funds but traded on stock exchanges like individual stocks. ETFs provide diversification and flexibility, making them ideal for long-term investments.

5. **Real Estate** – Property investments can include physical real estate (such as rental properties) or real estate investment trusts (REITs), which allow you to invest in real estate without owning physical properties.

Understanding these options is the first step to building a portfolio.

Investing is not a one-size-fits-all approach; it depends on factors like your financial goals, risk tolerance, and time horizon. If you're investing for a long-term goal like retirement, you can take on more risk, as you have time to ride out market fluctuations. For shorter-term goals, a conservative approach may be more suitable.

The Role of AI in Modern Investing

AI levels the playing field in investing.

AI's ability to analyze vast amounts of data, spot trends, and provide personalized recommendations has transformed the investing landscape. AI-powered platforms, known as robo-advisors, make it possible for beginners to access sophisticated investing strategies that were once available only to professional portfolio managers or high-net-worth individuals.

Some of the most popular AI-powered investing platforms include:

- **Betterment** and **Wealthfront** – These robo-advisors assess your financial goals, risk tolerance, and investment timeline, then create and manage a diversified portfolio for you. They automate everything from asset allocation to rebalancing and tax-loss harvesting, which optimizes your investment for tax efficiency.

- **Acorns** – This app is perfect for those starting small, as it automatically rounds up your purchases to the nearest dollar and invests the spare change. It's an effortless way to begin investing, especially if you're new to saving and investing.

- **Ellevest** – Targeted toward women, Ellevest offers personalized portfolios that consider women's unique financial circumstances, including gender-specific income patterns and life expectancy.

These platforms use AI algorithms to optimize investment choices based on individual preferences, minimizing risk and maximizing returns in alignment with your goals. With robo-advisors, you can start investing with as little as $10, and the technology will ensure your portfolio is tailored to your needs.

AI simplifies investing, making it easy to start and stay consistent.

Diversification: The Key to Reducing Risk

Don't put all your eggs in one basket.

One of the most important principles in investing is diversification, which means spreading your money across various assets to reduce risk. When you diversify, you're less vulnerable to the impact of any single investment's performance on your overall portfolio. For example, if you only invest in a single company's stock, you're exposed to significant risk if that company performs poorly. However, a diversified portfolio with stocks from multiple industries, bonds, and real estate can help cushion against market volatility.

AI-driven platforms are particularly skilled at creating diversified portfolios, as they can analyze vast amounts of data and identify asset correlations (the degree to which asset prices move together). Most robo-advisors automatically diversify your portfolio based on your risk tolerance, rebalancing it periodically to maintain your target asset allocation.

Diversification helps protect your investments while growing your wealth steadily.

Investing Strategies for Long-Term Growth

Long-term growth requires patience and strategy.

To build wealth, it's essential to adopt a strategy that aligns with your financial goals and time horizon. Here are a few common investment strategies that are particularly effective for long-term growth:

1. **Dollar-Cost Averaging (DCA)** – This approach involves investing a fixed amount of money at regular intervals, regardless of market conditions. By consistently investing, you buy more shares when prices are low and fewer when prices are high, potentially lowering your average cost per share over time. DCA is a great strategy for those who want to build wealth gradually without trying to time the market.

2. **Growth Investing** – Growth investors focus on stocks with high potential for appreciation, often in sectors like technology, healthcare, and renewable energy. While these investments can be more volatile, they offer significant growth potential over the long term.

3. **Income Investing** – This strategy prioritizes investments that generate regular income, such as dividend-paying stocks and bonds. It's a good choice for those who prefer a steady income stream and is often a component of retirement portfolios.

4. **Value Investing** – Popularized by investors like Warren Buffett, value investing involves seeking undervalued stocks with strong fundamentals. The goal is to buy stocks at a "discount" and hold them until they appreciate their intrinsic value.

5. **Index Investing** – Index funds and ETFs track the performance of a specific market index, like the S&P 500. This strategy offers diversification and typically involves lower fees, making it a cost-effective approach for long-term growth.

AI-driven platforms allow you to implement these strategies effortlessly. For example, Betterment offers both growth-focused and income-focused portfolios, automatically adjusting asset allocation based on your goals. With AI, you can easily experiment with different strategies and adapt your approach as your financial situation and goals evolve.

With AI, you can pursue growth without needing to be an expert.

Managing Risk and Staying Informed

Risk management is essential for confident investing.

Every investment carries some level of risk, and understanding how to manage it is crucial. While diversification helps mitigate risk, it's also essential to regularly review and adjust your portfolio, especially during market shifts. AI-driven platforms excel at risk management, as they continuously monitor and analyze market trends, allowing you to stay informed without dedicating hours to research.

Many apps, like Wealthfront and Betterment, adjust portfolios automatically to reduce risk as you near your investment goals. For example, if your goal is retirement, the platform may gradually shift from a growth-focused portfolio to a more conservative one as you approach retirement age. This process, known as "glide path," minimizes risk as you get closer to needing the funds.

AI takes the guesswork out of managing risk, so you can focus on the big picture.

Staying informed is another important aspect of confident investing. While AI tools do much of the heavy lifting, it's beneficial to keep a basic understanding of market trends, economic shifts, and investment performance. Apps like Finimize and Morningstar provide daily insights and market updates, making it easier to stay current without dedicating hours to research.

Knowledge is power—even small insights help you make smarter investment decisions.

The Importance of Discipline in Investing

Consistency is the backbone of successful investing.

Investing isn't about quick wins or overnight wealth—it's about steady, disciplined contributions that build up over time. Maintaining a disciplined approach means sticking with your strategy even when the market is volatile or when progress feels slow. This consistency allows you to take full advantage of market growth, weather economic downturns, and avoid the emotional decisions that lead to impulsive, risky moves.

For instance, during market downturns, the instinctive reaction is often to sell investments to avoid further losses. However, history shows that markets tend to recover, and those who stay invested typically benefit from the recovery. By remaining disciplined and sticking to your investment plan, you allow your portfolio to ride out fluctuations and capitalize on long-term gains.

AI-driven tools help reinforce this discipline by automating contributions, rebalancing portfolios, and sending reminders to keep you on track. Many platforms also offer "auto-reinvest" features, which reinvest dividends back into your portfolio, enhancing growth without requiring any action on your part.

Investing consistently, even in small amounts, leads to significant growth over time.

Leveraging Small Investments for Long-Term Growth

Small investments, when made consistently, yield powerful results.

One of the biggest barriers to investing is the misconception that you need a large amount of money to get started. The truth is that small, regular contributions can lead to substantial growth, thanks to the power of compounding. Compounding occurs when the returns you earn on your investments generate additional earnings, creating a snowball effect that grows your wealth faster over time.

Consider starting with an amount that's manageable within your budget. Even $10, $20, or $50 a month can make a significant difference over time. Many robo-advisors allow you to begin investing with as little as $10, making it easier than ever to get started. Acorns, for instance, rounds up your purchases to the nearest dollar and invests the difference, allowing you to build an investment portfolio without even noticing the contributions.

If you're able, gradually increase your monthly contributions as your income grows or expenses decrease. This approach not only amplifies the impact of compounding but also reinforces the habit of regular investing. AI-driven tools can simplify this process by allowing you to schedule incremental increases in your contributions, helping you steadily boost your investment rate without disrupting your budget.

Small steps toward investing today create a future of financial security and growth.

The Power of Compounding in Wealth-Building

Compounding is the secret to long-term financial independence.

Compounding is a cornerstone of wealth-building. It's the process by which the returns on your investments earn returns of their own, creating exponential growth over time. The longer you stay invested, the more significant the effect of compounding becomes, as each cycle of growth builds upon the last.

For example, if you invest $1,000 at a 7% annual return, that initial investment grows to $1,070 after one year. In the second year, you earn a return not just on the original $1,000 but also on the $70 in earnings, leading to even greater growth. Over decades, this cycle can transform even modest investments into substantial wealth.

Starting early and maintaining consistency are key to maximizing compounding. Even if you're in your 20s or 30s, starting with small contributions gives your money decades to grow. AI-driven tools support this by keeping your investments on track and reinvesting dividends automatically, ensuring that every dollar contributes to the compounding effect.

The earlier you start, the more powerful compounding becomes—time is your biggest asset.

Staying Focused on Your Investment Goals

Your goals are your compass in the world of investing.

Investing without a clear goal is like sailing without a destination. Defining your goals keeps you focused, helping you make decisions that align with your desired outcomes rather than reacting to short-term market changes. Investment goals can range from saving for retirement to building a down payment for a home, funding a child's education, or even generating passive income.

Once you've set your goals, use them as a guiding framework for your investment strategy. For example, if your goal is retirement, you may lean toward a growth-focused portfolio with a mix of stocks and ETFs. For shorter-term goals, a more conservative approach with bonds and high-yield savings accounts may be suitable.

AI platforms are excellent tools for staying aligned with your goals, as they can tailor portfolios specifically to your needs and track progress automatically. By regularly reviewing your goals and tracking your progress, you stay motivated and less likely to make impulsive investment choices.

Stay focused on your destination—short-term fluctuations won't deter you from long-term success.

Adjusting Your Investment Strategy Over Time

Financial independence is a dynamic journey—adjust as you grow.

As you move through different life stages, your financial goals and needs will likely change. The investment strategy you adopt in your 20s may not be ideal when you're nearing retirement. This evolution is natural, and adjusting your approach over time ensures your investments continue to support your changing lifestyle and aspirations.

For instance, younger investors often prioritize growth, with a larger proportion of their portfolio in stocks. As retirement approaches, many shift to a more conservative allocation to protect their gains. This gradual change in strategy, known as "glide path," can be automated with AI tools, which adjust your portfolio's risk profile as you near key milestones.

In addition to life stage adjustments, periodic reviews of your portfolio's performance allow you to make necessary changes. If certain investments underperform, it may be time to reallocate funds. Regular reviews ensure your portfolio remains optimized for growth, adapting to market changes and aligning with your evolving goals.

Investment strategies are flexible—adapt them to fit your life.

Embracing Patience and Long-Term Thinking

Patience is the greatest virtue in investing.

Successful investing requires patience and the ability to look beyond short-term market movements. The stock market will experience highs and lows, but these fluctuations don't determine your financial future. Instead of reacting to every dip or peak, adopt a long-term perspective. Historically, markets have trended upward over extended periods, rewarding those who stay invested.

When you feel uncertain, remember that the biggest gains often come from staying the course. For example, even during economic downturns, many successful investors, like Warren Buffett, have maintained their investments, trusting in market recovery. The discipline to hold investments despite temporary losses allows compounding to work its magic, turning initial investments into substantial wealth over time.

AI tools also help in maintaining this discipline, as many platforms use automated algorithms that eliminate emotional decision-making, encouraging you to stick to your plan.

Long-term thinking transforms volatility into opportunity.

Embracing a Balanced Approach with AI

Balance creates resilience in any investment portfolio.

While growth-focused investments like stocks are essential for wealth building, a balanced approach that includes bonds, real estate, and other assets reduces risk. This diversification not only stabilizes your portfolio but also prepares you to weather different economic cycles.

AI-driven platforms simplify balanced investing by managing asset allocation, rebalancing portfolios, and recommending adjustments based on market conditions. They monitor your portfolio's risk and automatically make changes to maintain balance, helping you achieve both growth and security. This approach ensures that your portfolio remains resilient, growing steadily without exposing you to unnecessary risk.

With AI as your ally, balance becomes an effortless part of your investing strategy, allowing you to focus on growth while safeguarding your investments.

Balanced portfolios endure and grow, even through turbulent times.

Final Thoughts on Investing with Confidence

Confident investing is within everyone's reach.

Investing is a critical step toward financial independence, but it doesn't have to be complicated or intimidating. With a clear understanding of basic investment principles, a disciplined approach, and the support of AI-driven tools, anyone can build a strong, growth-focused portfolio.

Start with small contributions, stay consistent, and let the power of compounding work in your favor.

As you build your investment portfolio, remember that financial independence is a long-term goal. The steps you take today will set the foundation for a future of freedom, stability, and choice. By embracing patience, maintaining focus on your goals, and using technology to simplify and optimize your strategy, you're well on your way to achieving lasting wealth.

Your journey to financial independence starts with confidence and consistency—invest in both.

Chapter – 8:
Diversifying Income Streams

Financial independence isn't about one income stream; it's about building multiple pathways to wealth.

One of the core principles of financial independence is the ability to generate income from various sources. Relying solely on a single paycheck or income stream leaves you vulnerable to economic changes, job loss, or industry shifts. Diversifying your income not only provides a safety net but also accelerates your journey toward financial independence by allowing you to earn, save, and invest more.

Creating multiple income streams may seem challenging, but today's technology, particularly AI, has opened up countless opportunities. Whether you're interested in freelance work, investing, side businesses, or passive income sources, there are ways to build extra income that align with your skills and goals. This chapter will explore various income sources, show you how to get started, and demonstrate how AI can simplify and optimize the process of diversifying your income.

Multiple income streams make financial independence resilient and attainable.

Why Diversify Your Income?

Diversification protects and empowers.

The concept of diversification applies to more than just investing—it's crucial for income generation as well. Having multiple income streams provides security, as it reduces dependence on any one source of income. If one stream is disrupted, others can help sustain your lifestyle and financial goals.

Here are some compelling reasons to diversify:

1. **Risk Management**: A diversified income protects you from economic downturns, job losses, and industry-specific declines. If one stream dries up, the others can cover your basic needs.

2. **Faster Wealth Accumulation**: More income streams mean more money to save and invest, speeding up your journey to financial independence.

3. **Skill Development**: Exploring different income streams often involves learning new skills, which can enhance your primary career or open new professional doors.

4. **Financial Freedom and Flexibility**: With diversified income, you're not tied to a single job or location. This freedom allows you to make choices based on what aligns with your values, rather than financial necessity.

Diversifying income isn't just about making money—it's about creating financial security and choice.

Active Income Streams: Freelancing and Side Hustles

Active income streams are where skills meet opportunity.

Active income requires your time and effort. Freelancing, consulting, and side hustles are common ways to generate additional income, especially if you have a skill or service that's in demand. With AI platforms like Upwork, Fiverr, and TaskRabbit, connecting with potential clients has become easier and more accessible, even if you're new to freelancing.

Freelancing Opportunities

Freelancing can include a wide range of skills—from writing and graphic design to programming and marketing. Sites like Upwork and Fiverr allow you to showcase your skills, set your rates, and connect with clients looking for specific services. Additionally, AI algorithms help match you with relevant projects, increasing your chances of finding gigs that align with your expertise.

1. **Writing and Content Creation**: Businesses are constantly in need of content for websites, blogs, and social media. If you have strong writing skills, freelancing as a content writer or copywriter can be a lucrative side income.

2. **Graphic Design and Multimedia**: Graphic designers, video editors, and photographers have ample opportunities to earn extra income through platforms like Fiverr. AI tools like Canva and Adobe Spark simplify the design process, even for those new to the field.

3. **Programming and IT Services**: With the tech industry's rapid growth, programming and IT support are in high demand. Freelancing as a developer, data analyst, or cybersecurity consultant can significantly boost your income, especially if you use platforms like Upwork.

4. **Tutoring and Consulting**: If you have expertise in a specific subject or industry, consider tutoring or consulting. Sites like Preply for language tutoring or Clarity.fm for consulting make it easy to connect with clients who need your knowledge.

Freelancing lets you monetize your skills, creating an active income stream beyond your main job.

Starting a Side Hustle

A side hustle is a venture you can run outside your main job. Unlike freelancing, side hustles can sometimes evolve into passive income sources if structured well. For instance, selling digital products, running an online store, or creating a niche blog with affiliate links are side hustles that can eventually generate income with minimal ongoing effort.

Examples of side hustles include:

- **Selling Digital Products**: If you have expertise in a subject, consider creating and selling digital products like e-books, templates, or online courses. AI tools like ChatGPT can assist in content creation, while platforms like Gumroad or Etsy help distribute your products.

- **Dropshipping**: Running a dropshipping business involves selling products online without holding inventory. Platforms like Shopify integrate with suppliers, and AI tools can help you identify trending products and manage customer inquiries.

- **Affiliate Marketing**: Affiliate marketing involves promoting products and earning a commission on sales made through your links. Niche blogging, social media, and email newsletters can be powerful channels for affiliate marketing. With AI-driven keyword research tools, you can optimize content for higher engagement and income.

Side hustles are flexible ways to diversify income—start small, then scale up.

Passive Income Streams: Making Money Work for You

Passive income is the ultimate goal of financial independence.

Unlike active income, passive income requires an upfront investment of time, money, or resources but generates returns with minimal ongoing effort. Passive income streams allow you to make money while focusing on other things, making them ideal for those aiming for financial freedom.

Investing in Dividend Stocks

One of the most popular forms of passive income is dividend investing. By purchasing shares of companies that pay dividends, you earn a regular income based on the number of shares you hold. Many blue-chip stocks—such as those from established companies in industries like finance, utilities, and consumer goods—offer consistent dividends, making them reliable sources of passive income.

AI-powered investment platforms, like Betterment and Wealthfront, help investors select dividend stocks aligned with their financial goals. These platforms automatically reinvest dividends, compounding your income over time without additional effort.

Real Estate and REITs

Real estate has long been a preferred method for generating passive income. While buying physical property can be capital-intensive, Real Estate Investment Trusts (REITs) offer a more accessible way to invest in real estate. REITs pool investor funds to buy and manage properties, distributing profits to investors in the form of dividends.

Platforms like Fundrise and RealtyMogul use AI to analyze property markets, assess potential investments, and manage portfolios. With as little as $500, you can start investing in real estate through REITs, gaining exposure to property income without the need for hands-on management.

Real estate remains a cornerstone of passive income—REITs make it accessible for everyone.

Peer-to-Peer Lending

Peer-to-peer (P2P) lending allows individuals to lend money directly to borrowers, earning interest on their investments. Platforms like Prosper and LendingClub connect lenders and borrowers, using AI to assess credit risk and match loans with appropriate investors.

While P2P lending carries some risk, as borrowers may default, AI algorithms help reduce this by evaluating borrower profiles and assigning risk ratings. By diversifying across multiple loans, lenders can mitigate risk and enjoy steady passive income.

P2P lending turns your money into an asset, earning interest with minimal involvement.

Creating Digital Products for Recurring Revenue

Digital products, like e-books, online courses, or software, are excellent sources of passive income. Once created, these products require little maintenance and can be sold repeatedly. Platforms like Teachable for courses and Amazon Kindle Direct Publishing for e-books provide straightforward distribution channels, while AI tools can aid in the creation process.

For example, if you're skilled in graphic design, consider selling templates on Etsy or Creative Market. AI design tools, like Canva and Adobe Spark, can speed up the process and enhance your products, making it easy to create appealing templates that customers will pay for.

Digital products offer recurring revenue with minimal upkeep—create once, earn repeatedly.

Exploring Additional Passive Income Ideas

The more passive income streams you create, the closer you are to financial freedom.

Passive income allows you to earn money with minimal ongoing effort, making it one of the most effective tools for financial independence. Here are some more ideas for creating passive income that can support your goals:

Licensing Your Creative Work

If you're an artist, writer, photographer, or musician, licensing your creative work can be a valuable source of passive income. Licensing means granting permission for others to use your work while earning a fee or royalty in return. Platforms like Shutterstock for photography, Spotify and Apple Music for music, and Kindle Direct Publishing for ebooks enable creators to earn royalties whenever their work is downloaded or used.

AI tools like DALL-E for digital art or ChatGPT for writing can help creators streamline their work processes, making it easier to produce high-quality content. By building a portfolio of licensed work, you can develop a steady income stream that grows with your creative output.

Your creativity can become a recurring revenue source when licensed effectively.

Developing an App or Website

Creating an app or a website that generates income through ads, subscriptions, or affiliate marketing is another way to earn passive income. While building an app or website requires upfront work, it can produce ongoing revenue once it's live and attracts visitors.

Today, you don't need extensive coding skills to create an app or website. Platforms like WordPress, Wix, or Shopify offer user-friendly tools, and AI services like ChatGPT can help generate content, while AI-powered design tools create visually appealing layouts. You can monetize your site or app through Google AdSense, affiliate links, or selling your own digital products.

Apps and websites can become assets that earn income around the clock.

Investing in High-Yield Savings Accounts or CDs

For those who prefer low-risk investments, high-yield savings accounts (HYSA) and Certificates of Deposit (CDs) are viable options for passive income. While they don't offer high returns, they provide steady, predictable growth, ideal for emergency funds or short-term savings goals.

Many online banks offer HYSAs that provide higher interest rates than traditional savings accounts. CDs, on the other hand, offer fixed interest rates for a set period, making them ideal for people who won't need to access these funds for a while. AI tools can track interest rate trends and recommend HYSAs or CDs with the highest returns, helping you optimize even low-risk investments.

HYSAs and CDs are safe ways to grow savings without added risk.

Managing Multiple Income Streams Efficiently

Efficiency is key when balancing multiple income sources.

As you build and diversify your income streams, managing each one can become complex, especially if you're balancing active and passive sources. Efficient management ensures that each stream contributes to your financial goals without overwhelming you. Here are some strategies to keep things streamlined:

Using AI-Driven Financial Management Tools

AI-powered financial management tools like Mint, Personal Capital, and QuickBooks make tracking multiple income streams simpler and more organized. These apps provide a consolidated view of all your accounts, allowing you to track income, expenses, and investments from one dashboard. They categorize income sources automatically, so you can see how much each stream contributes to your total cash flow.

For business-related income, QuickBooks and FreshBooks are valuable for managing finances, tracking expenses, and preparing for tax season. AI simplifies accounting by automating expense tracking, generating financial reports, and even predicting cash flow based on historical data.

AI-powered tools keep your financial ecosystem organized and efficient.

Automating Contributions to Savings and Investments

To maximize the benefits of your multiple income streams, automate contributions to your savings and investment accounts. For instance, if you have a main job, a side hustle, and passive income from dividends, set up automatic transfers from each source into a high-yield savings or brokerage account. This way, a portion of every dollar earned works toward growing your wealth.

For example, you could allocate 20% of each income stream to savings and investments. By automating these transfers, you ensure that each stream contributes consistently, building momentum toward financial independence.

Automation keeps your financial goals on track, even with varied income.

Setting Up a Budget for Each Income Stream

Budgeting for each income stream separately helps you understand how much each one contributes to your overall financial picture. For example, if your side hustle covers your entertainment expenses while your main job covers essentials and savings, you gain better control over your finances.

AI-driven budgeting apps like YNAB or PocketGuard can help you categorize expenses and income sources, allowing you to create a clear budget for each stream. By budgeting according to each income source, you reduce the risk of overspending and ensure that every dollar aligns with your goals.

Separate budgets make managing multiple income streams simple and effective.

Prioritizing High-Return Streams

As you develop multiple income streams, some will naturally yield higher returns than others. By prioritizing the ones that provide the most significant benefits, you can maximize your income potential without spreading yourself too thin.

For example, if a side business is generating substantial income and has potential for growth, consider investing more time or resources into it. Conversely, if a stream like P2P lending is lower-yielding or high-risk, you may allocate less time or reduce your investment in that area.

Focus your efforts where the returns are strongest for optimal growth.

How AI Can Help Optimize Your Income Strategy

AI turns income diversification from complex to convenient.

AI tools simplify the process of managing and optimizing multiple income streams by providing insights, automating tasks, and identifying trends. Here's how AI can help:

1. **Identifying New Income Opportunities**: Platforms like Fiverr and Upwork use AI to match freelancers with jobs, while marketplaces like Etsy and Amazon offer analytics to show trending products. These insights help you identify profitable areas to explore.

2. **Improving Cash Flow with Predictive Analytics**: AI-driven financial platforms can analyze cash flow patterns and predict periods of low or high income. For example, if you're a freelancer with seasonal income, predictive analytics can help you prepare for leaner months by suggesting savings targets or expense adjustments.

3. **Enhancing Productivity with AI-Powered Tools**: AI tools streamline the workload involved in running side hustles or small businesses. Apps like Grammarly, Canva, and Hootsuite help create content, design visuals, and schedule social media posts, reducing the time required to manage business operations.

4. **Optimizing Investment Portfolios**: Robo-advisors like Wealthfront and Betterment use AI to diversify and manage investment portfolios based on your goals and risk tolerance. By automating investment management, they allow you to grow wealth from dividends or market gains without actively overseeing your portfolio.

AI maximizes efficiency, so every income stream runs smoothly and effectively.

Balancing Active and Passive Income Streams

Active and passive income work together to accelerate financial independence.

While active income requires your time and effort, passive income continues to generate revenue even when you're not actively involved. Balancing both types is essential for financial resilience and accelerated wealth-building. Active income from side hustles, freelancing, or consulting provides immediate cash flow, while passive income from investments or digital products contributes to long-term stability.

Consider setting a target ratio between active and passive income. For example, you may aim for a 70/30 split, with 70% coming from passive sources as you approach financial independence. By gradually increasing your passive income, you reduce your reliance on active sources over time, moving closer to the freedom that financial independence offers.

The right balance of active and passive income creates a stable, sustainable path to wealth.

Monitoring and Adjusting Your Income Strategy

Regular reviews ensure your income strategy evolves with you.

Your financial goals and needs will change over time, making it essential to periodically review and adjust your income strategy. Monitor each stream's performance, evaluate growth potential, and decide if adjustments are necessary. For instance, if a side hustle has become too demanding without yielding significant returns, consider shifting focus to more profitable or passive sources.

AI tools, like Mint or Personal Capital, offer features that allow you to track income and spending trends, helping you make informed decisions. Regular reviews keep your strategy aligned with your evolving goals, ensuring you stay on course toward financial independence.

Financial independence requires adaptability—adjust your strategy as needed.

Final Thoughts on Diversifying Income Streams

Diversified income is a powerful tool for financial independence.

Building multiple income streams is a dynamic approach to achieving financial independence, providing security, flexibility, and accelerated growth. With the help of AI tools, managing and optimizing these streams becomes simpler and more efficient, allowing you to maximize your financial potential with less effort.

As you continue on your journey, remember that every income stream you create brings you closer to your vision of financial freedom. By balancing active and passive income sources, automating your finances, and using AI to streamline your efforts, you're crafting a robust and resilient financial future.

Multiple streams of income empower you to live a life defined by freedom, security, and choice.

Chapter – 9:
Cultivating a Resilient Mindset for Financial Independence

Financial independence starts in the mind—it's a journey shaped by resilience.

Achieving financial independence isn't just about managing money or creating income streams; it's about developing a mindset that supports your goals. The path to financial freedom is filled with ups and downs, from market fluctuations to unexpected expenses, and even moments of self-doubt. Building a resilient mindset prepares you to handle these challenges, adapt to changes, and stay committed to your vision.

This chapter will explore the importance of resilience, patience, and discipline, as well as how to build these qualities into your financial journey. Developing the right mindset not only empowers you to face financial obstacles but also allows you to enjoy the journey, celebrate progress, and stay motivated even when things don't go as planned.

Resilience is the foundation on which financial freedom is built.

Embracing Patience as a Key to Long-Term Success

Patience is a powerful financial tool.

In a world driven by instant gratification, patience can feel like a rare and difficult quality to cultivate. But in the context of financial independence, patience is essential. Building wealth and achieving financial independence is a gradual process, requiring consistent effort over years, or even decades. When you embrace patience, you allow your investments to grow, your savings to accumulate, and your efforts to compound, creating the foundation for financial freedom.

Investing, in particular, requires patience. Market volatility can be unsettling, especially for new investors, but successful wealth-building hinges on the ability to stay invested despite fluctuations. The temptation to sell investments during market downturns can be strong, yet staying the course often leads to better outcomes. History shows that markets generally trend upward over time, rewarding those who have the patience to wait.

Patience turns market fluctuations into opportunities for long-term growth.

Patience is also crucial in debt repayment. Paying off debt, especially high-interest debt, can take time and dedication. Instead of focusing on the time it takes to eliminate debt, celebrate small milestones along the way—like paying off a single credit card or reducing the principal of a loan. By taking it step-by-step, you build patience into your journey, making it easier to stay motivated.

With patience, even the longest journey becomes achievable.

Developing Financial Discipline

Discipline is the fuel that drives financial progress.

Financial discipline is the ability to make consistent, intentional choices that align with your long-term goals, even when it's difficult. Discipline is what keeps you from overspending on wants rather than needs, sticking to a budget, and prioritizing saving and investing over impulsive purchases. It's what empowers you to make sacrifices today for greater financial security tomorrow.

Discipline can be built gradually, starting with small habits. If budgeting is new to you, begin by tracking a single spending category, such as dining out or entertainment. Once you're comfortable, expand your tracking to other areas. Similarly, if saving feels challenging, start with a manageable amount each month, and increase it as you gain confidence. Over time, these habits build into a strong foundation of discipline.

Financial discipline turns dreams of independence into concrete goals.

AI-powered tools can support your discipline by automating aspects of your financial plan. For instance, automating transfers to savings or investments ensures that you're prioritizing your financial goals consistently, reducing the temptation to spend impulsively. Apps like YNAB or Mint can provide reminders when you approach budget limits, reinforcing your spending discipline.

Technology strengthens discipline by keeping you accountable.

Building Resilience in the Face of Setbacks

Resilience allows you to face setbacks without losing sight of your goals.

Every journey to financial independence encounters setbacks, whether they come in the form of unexpected expenses, economic downturns, or personal challenges. Resilience is the mental and emotional strength to recover from these setbacks, adapt to changes, and continue moving forward. Rather than viewing obstacles as roadblocks, resilience helps you see them as opportunities to learn and grow.

Building resilience begins with a mindset shift. Instead of expecting a perfectly smooth path, acknowledge that challenges are a natural part of the process. This perspective enables you to handle setbacks with patience and adaptability. For example, if you encounter an emergency expense that temporarily derails your savings plan, resilience allows you to adjust your timeline and get back on track when possible.

Resilience turns obstacles into stepping stones.

One practical way to build resilience is by maintaining an emergency fund. A well-funded emergency account provides a buffer, allowing you to handle unexpected expenses without compromising your financial goals. Even a small emergency fund can reduce financial stress and provide peace of mind, empowering you to tackle challenges with greater confidence.

An emergency fund is a tool for financial resilience.

Adapting to Life's Changes with Flexibility

Flexibility is essential for navigating life's inevitable changes.

Financial independence is not a rigid goal—it's a journey that must adapt to different stages of life. Changes in career, family, health, or personal priorities can impact your financial situation and require you to adjust your strategy. Flexibility is the ability to pivot and adjust your goals or timeline as needed, while still staying aligned with your vision of independence.

For instance, a job change might alter your income or require relocation expenses. Instead of seeing this as a setback, a flexible mindset allows you to temporarily adjust spending, focus on building savings, or explore new income streams. Flexibility ensures that you remain committed to your goals without feeling restricted by a single approach.

With flexibility, every change becomes a new opportunity for growth.

Adaptability is also valuable in investment strategy. As your financial situation and risk tolerance evolve, so too might your investment preferences. Young investors may prioritize high-growth assets, while those nearing retirement might prefer conservative options. By periodically reviewing your goals and adjusting your portfolio, you ensure that your investments align with your current stage in life.

Adapting to change strengthens your resilience and commitment to financial freedom.

Embracing Delayed Gratification

Delayed gratification is the path to lasting wealth.

Delayed gratification is the ability to prioritize long-term rewards over short-term pleasures. It's about choosing to save or invest today rather than spending on immediate wants. Practicing delayed gratification doesn't mean denying yourself all pleasures; it means making intentional decisions about when to spend and when to save, knowing that each choice brings you closer to financial independence.

For example, instead of purchasing a luxury item on impulse, consider saving for it gradually or setting a savings target before indulging. This approach allows you to enjoy the reward without compromising your financial goals. Delayed gratification also strengthens your resilience by reinforcing your ability to prioritize future rewards over immediate satisfaction.

Choosing future freedom over present convenience builds a foundation for wealth.

Delayed gratification plays a significant role in saving for large goals, such as retirement or a down payment on a house. By consistently putting aside money for these long-term goals, you create a financial cushion that offers security and freedom. This practice not only benefits your finances but also builds discipline and resilience, making you better equipped to stay focused on your objectives.

Patience today ensures abundance tomorrow.

Staying Focused on Your Vision

Your vision is your compass on the journey to financial independence.

Having a clear vision of your financial goals is essential for staying motivated and resilient. When you know why you're working toward financial independence—whether it's to achieve a specific lifestyle, provide for loved ones, or simply enjoy freedom—you have a powerful motivator that guides your decisions. This vision acts as a compass, helping you navigate challenges, resist distractions, and stay focused on what truly matters.

Write down your vision or create a vision board that represents your financial goals. Include images, words, or symbols that remind you of your dreams and ambitions. Place it somewhere visible to keep your goals front and center, especially when faced with tough decisions or setbacks.

Your vision keeps you grounded, reminding you why you're committed to financial freedom.

Regularly revisiting your vision also allows you to adjust it as your life evolves. Goals may change as you grow and experience new things. By periodically reflecting on your vision, you stay aligned with your deepest values and aspirations, ensuring that your financial journey remains fulfilling and purpose-driven.

Stay connected to your vision—it's the fuel that powers your journey.

Celebrating Small Wins to Build Motivation

Small victories keep the fire burning on the road to financial independence.

The journey to financial freedom is long, and staying motivated over time can be challenging. One way to keep your spirits high is by celebrating small milestones. Recognizing these achievements reinforces your commitment, giving you the momentum to keep going even when the ultimate goal feels distant.

Celebrating small wins doesn't have to be extravagant. It can be as simple as treating yourself to a favorite meal, a night off from responsibilities, or a new book you've wanted to read. For instance, if you reach a savings target, acknowledge it and savor the progress. These celebrations are reminders that every step forward, no matter how small, contributes to your larger vision.

Acknowledging small wins builds confidence and keeps you moving forward.

A practical way to track your progress is by setting up a milestone system. Break your main financial goals into smaller, achievable steps. For example, if you aim to save $10,000, set mini-goals at $1,000, $2,500, $5,000, and so on. Each time you hit a milestone, celebrate in a way that motivates you to reach the next. This approach helps you stay focused, creating a sense of progress that reinforces your efforts.

Celebrating small wins turns long-term goals into a series of rewarding moments.

Using Positive Reinforcement to Maintain Discipline

Positive reinforcement strengthens financial habits and discipline.

Positive reinforcement is a powerful psychological tool for building resilience and discipline. By rewarding yourself for making good financial choices, you reinforce behaviors that support your goals. This approach turns budgeting, saving, and disciplined spending into habits that feel rewarding rather than restrictive.

For instance, each month you stick to your budget, consider allocating a small "reward fund" for something enjoyable. Over time, this positive association makes budgeting less of a chore and more of a fulfilling habit. Likewise, if you resist an impulse buy, congratulate yourself on the strength it took to stay focused on your priorities.

Rewarding good habits turns financial discipline into a source of pride and motivation.

AI-driven budgeting tools can support positive reinforcement by offering insights and reminders. Apps like Mint or YNAB often provide progress reports, showing how much you've saved over time. Seeing these results reinforces your efforts, reminding you of the progress made by sticking to your financial plan.

Tracking progress with technology boosts morale and keeps you disciplined.

Practicing Gratitude to Foster a Positive Mindset

Gratitude transforms your perspective on money and goals.

Practicing gratitude is a powerful way to maintain a positive and resilient mindset. Financial independence is as much about appreciating what you have as it is about pursuing more. When you regularly reflect on what you're grateful for—whether it's financial stability, loved ones, or opportunities—you cultivate a mindset of abundance rather than scarcity.

One way to practice gratitude is by keeping a gratitude journal. Take a few minutes each day or week to jot down things you appreciate. They don't have to be grand gestures; even small things, like enjoying a debt-free day or sticking to your budget, are worth celebrating. Over time, this habit reshapes your outlook, making it easier to stay resilient through challenges.

Gratitude creates a mindset of abundance, turning every step forward into a celebration.

Another approach is to include "gratitude moments" in your financial routine. For example, after each budgeting session or financial review, take a minute to reflect on what your financial journey has allowed you to achieve so far. This practice helps you stay focused on your progress rather than dwelling on what remains to be done.

Gratitude shifts focus from what's missing to what's already achieved.

Learning from Setbacks as Part of the Journey

Setbacks are opportunities to learn and grow.

Setbacks are inevitable on the road to financial independence, but they don't have to derail your progress. Instead of seeing setbacks as failures, view them as learning experiences. Each challenge you encounter offers insight into your habits, weaknesses, or areas for improvement. With this perspective, setbacks become stepping stones rather than roadblocks.

For instance, if an unexpected expense temporarily disrupts your savings plan, take the time to analyze what happened. Did you overlook an area in your budget? Was the expense something that could be planned for in the future? By understanding the cause of the setback, you can take steps to prevent similar situations in the future, making your financial plan even stronger.

Learning from setbacks makes your journey more resilient and adaptable.

AI-powered financial apps can help identify patterns in spending or savings that lead to setbacks. For example, apps like Truebill and Mint can alert you to recurring expenses you might have missed, giving you the insight to adjust your budget accordingly. Using technology to learn from setbacks not only simplifies the process but also strengthens your overall approach to financial management.

Setbacks teach resilience—embrace them as valuable lessons.

Cultivating a Long-Term Perspective

Financial independence is a marathon, not a sprint.

A long-term perspective is essential for maintaining resilience in your financial journey. Financial independence is rarely achieved overnight; it requires years of planning, saving, investing, and discipline. By focusing on the long-term benefits rather than short-term gains, you create a mindset that supports sustained progress.

One effective way to maintain a long-term perspective is to focus on the lifestyle you're building rather than the sacrifices you're making. For example, every dollar saved today brings you closer to a future where financial stress is minimized. By keeping this bigger picture in mind, you can more easily stay committed to your goals, even when faced with temptations or setbacks.

Long-term focus turns everyday decisions into investments in your future.

Visualizing your life at financial independence can also strengthen this perspective. Imagine the freedom, security, and choices that come with being financially independent. Keeping this vision alive serves as a reminder of why you're putting in the effort now, reinforcing your dedication to the journey.

Hold your vision close—it's the compass that guides you through challenges.

Surrounding Yourself with Supportive Influences

Positive influences reinforce your financial journey.

The people you surround yourself with have a significant impact on your mindset and motivation. Connecting with others who share similar financial goals or values can make your journey more enjoyable and less isolating. These relationships offer encouragement, accountability, and shared wisdom, especially during challenging times.

Consider joining a community, online or in person, that focuses on financial independence. Platforms like Reddit's r/financialindependence or various personal finance forums provide a space to share progress, ask for advice, and celebrate wins with others on similar paths. Additionally, reading about others' success stories or struggles can inspire you to stay committed.

Supportive communities make the journey to financial independence a shared experience.

Mentorship is another valuable resource. If you know someone who has achieved financial independence, ask for guidance or advice. Mentors can offer insights based on their experiences, helping you avoid common pitfalls and approach challenges more strategically.

With the right influences, every step forward feels supported and encouraged.

Finding Balance Between Discipline and Enjoyment

Balance is the key to sustainable financial freedom.

While discipline and sacrifice are essential to financial independence, it's equally important to find joy along the way. An overly restrictive approach can lead to burnout, making it harder to maintain momentum over the long term. By balancing discipline with moments of enjoyment, you create a sustainable, fulfilling journey that you're more likely to stick with.

Incorporate "fun" categories into your budget that allow you to indulge occasionally without guilt. Set aside a portion of your budget for experiences or small luxuries that bring you happiness. These planned indulgences prevent feelings of deprivation and make the financial journey more enjoyable.

Enjoying the journey keeps you motivated to reach your destination.

By finding balance, you remind yourself that financial independence isn't just about reaching a goal; it's about creating a life that's satisfying and fulfilling at every stage. This mindset fosters resilience, allowing you to prioritize both your present well-being and your future security.

Balance turns financial freedom into a journey of both discipline and delight.

Final Thoughts on Building a Resilient Mindset

Resilience is the foundation of a financially independent life.

Building a resilient mindset is essential for anyone pursuing financial independence. Through patience, discipline, adaptability, and gratitude, you develop the mental strength to navigate challenges, maintain motivation, and stay focused on your goals. This resilience allows you to not only reach financial independence but also to enjoy the journey along the way.

As you continue, remember that resilience is not a one-time achievement—it's a quality you cultivate with each step. Every setback overcome, every small victory celebrated, and every choice made with intention strengthens your commitment to financial independence. By nurturing a resilient mindset, you're setting yourself up for a future defined by freedom, fulfillment, and the ability to navigate life on your terms.

Resilience transforms financial goals into a reality. Cultivate it, embrace it, and let it lead you to financial freedom.

Chapter – 10:
Planning for the Future – Ensuring Lasting Financial Independence

Financial independence isn't a destination; it's a lifelong journey.

Achieving financial independence is an incredible accomplishment, but maintaining it over the years requires careful planning and adaptability. Long-term financial stability doesn't just happen; it's the result of ongoing effort, disciplined saving, and strategic planning that anticipates future needs and changes. Chapter 10 focuses on the crucial steps needed to sustain financial freedom well into the future, including retirement planning, estate management, and building a legacy for the next generation.

Planning for the future is about more than securing your own comfort—it's about preparing for life's uncertainties and ensuring that your financial success positively impacts those around you. With careful planning, you can enjoy a fulfilling retirement, provide for loved ones, and leave a lasting impact.

Long-term planning transforms financial independence from a goal into a legacy.

Retirement Planning: Securing a Comfortable Future

Retirement isn't an end; it's the beginning of a new chapter.

Retirement planning is one of the most significant components of long-term financial planning. It's about ensuring that the income generated from your savings and investments will support your lifestyle when you're no longer actively working. For those who achieve financial independence early, retirement doesn't necessarily mean stopping work entirely; it might mean having the freedom to pursue passion projects, volunteer, or start new ventures without the need for a paycheck.

Start by estimating your retirement needs based on your current lifestyle and anticipated changes. Consider factors like:

1. **Lifestyle Costs**: How much will you need to maintain your desired lifestyle? Remember to account for hobbies, travel, and other interests you plan to pursue in retirement.

2. **Healthcare**: Medical expenses typically increase with age, so including healthcare costs is essential. Look into long-term care insurance or health savings accounts (HSAs) to cover future healthcare needs.

3. **Inflation**: Over time, the cost of living will likely rise, impacting the purchasing power of your savings. To combat this, consider investments that grow at or above the rate of inflation, like stocks or real estate.

4. **Lifespan**: Plan for a longer retirement than expected, as people are living longer today. Aiming for 30 years of retirement funding is a safe approach, with provisions for potential emergencies or extended healthcare needs.

Retirement planning provides a roadmap to a fulfilling, worry-free future.

Robo-advisors and AI-driven financial planning tools make it easier to estimate and save for retirement. Tools like Wealthfront, Betterment, and Fidelity Retirement Planner analyze your current savings, investment returns, and expenses to provide a retirement target and recommend monthly contributions. These platforms offer simulations that help you understand how your savings will grow over time and how adjustments in contributions or spending can impact your retirement fund.

Technology simplifies retirement planning, allowing you to focus on the future.

Sustainable Withdrawal Strategies

Once you reach retirement, managing withdrawals from your retirement accounts is crucial to ensure your savings last as long as needed. The traditional "4% rule" suggests withdrawing 4% of your retirement savings each year, adjusted for inflation, which has historically provided a safe income stream while preserving principal. However, this rule may not be suitable for everyone, especially in times of economic uncertainty or lower-than-average investment returns.

To develop a withdrawal strategy that aligns with your needs, consider these factors:

1. **Market Conditions**: In years when the market performs well, you may withdraw slightly more, while in down years, consider adjusting to a lower rate.

2. **Income Sources**: If you have other income sources, like rental income, pensions, or Social Security, you may reduce the amount withdrawn from retirement accounts.

3. **Flexible Withdrawals**: Adjusting withdrawals based on spending needs and market performance allows you to preserve your principal and extend the life of your savings.

4. **Tax Efficiency**: Withdrawals from different types of accounts (e.g., Roth IRA, traditional IRA, 401(k)) have different tax implications. Working with a financial advisor or using AI-driven tax planning tools can help optimize withdrawals to minimize tax liabilities.

Sustainable withdrawals protect your retirement fund, ensuring it supports you throughout your life.

Withdrawing from retirement accounts requires a balance between meeting current needs and preserving future income. A gradual, flexible approach ensures you won't exhaust your savings early in retirement. AI-powered tools, like Vanguard's retirement calculators, can assist by simulating different withdrawal rates and showing how long your money will last based on various scenarios.

Estate Planning: Leaving a Legacy

Planning for the future includes providing for loved ones.

Estate planning is essential for ensuring that your assets are distributed according to your wishes and that your loved ones are cared for. Effective estate planning allows you to leave a legacy, ease the financial burden on your family, and prevent disputes over asset distribution.

An estate plan typically includes a will, power of attorney, and possibly a trust. Here's a breakdown of these elements:

1. **Will**: A will specifies how you want your assets distributed upon your passing. It's a fundamental document for anyone with dependents or significant assets.

2. **Power of Attorney**: Assigning power of attorney allows someone you trust to manage your financial and healthcare decisions if you become unable to do so.

3. **Trusts**: Trusts offer more control over asset distribution, especially if you want to set specific conditions on how assets are used. They're useful tools for reducing estate taxes and ensuring privacy.

4. **Beneficiaries**: Designate beneficiaries for retirement accounts, life insurance policies, and other accounts to streamline asset distribution.

5. **Living Will**: This document outlines your preferences for end-of-life care, providing guidance to loved ones during difficult times.

Estate planning ensures your legacy aligns with your values and intentions.

AI and online tools simplify estate planning. Platforms like Trust & Will and LegalZoom guide you through creating a will or establishing a trust, providing templates and expert assistance at a lower cost than traditional estate planning services. Many of these services allow you to update documents as your circumstances change, making estate planning an ongoing part of your financial independence journey.

Estate planning is a proactive way to care for loved ones, even when you're gone.

Building a Legacy Beyond Finances

Your legacy is more than wealth; it's the impact you leave behind.

Leaving a legacy isn't solely about money—it's about the values, skills, and lessons you pass down to future generations. As you plan for your financial future, consider ways to share your knowledge and values with those who will carry on after you.

Mentorship, education, and sharing stories of your financial journey can have a lasting impact. For example, teaching children or younger family members about budgeting, saving, and investing equips them to make informed financial decisions. Documenting your experiences and the lessons learned along the way can inspire and guide others, turning your legacy into a source of empowerment.

Your legacy lives in the knowledge, values, and inspiration you share.

Preparing for Healthcare Costs in Retirement

Healthcare planning is essential for lasting financial security.

One of the most significant expenses retirees face is healthcare, which tends to increase with age. Without proper planning, medical expenses can deplete retirement savings, making it essential to include healthcare as a core part of your financial independence plan. Preparing for these expenses helps protect your financial security and gives you peace of mind as you age.

Health Savings Accounts (HSAs)

Health Savings Accounts (HSAs) are a valuable tool for those who are eligible. Contributions to HSAs are tax-deductible, and the funds can grow tax-free if used for qualifying medical expenses. Additionally, HSAs can serve as a tax-advantaged savings vehicle in retirement, especially if you delay withdrawals until later in life, allowing for long-term growth.

To maximize an HSA, contribute the maximum allowable amount each year, invest the funds in diversified assets, and try to cover current healthcare expenses out of pocket if possible. This allows your HSA to grow, creating a financial buffer for future healthcare needs.

An HSA is a triple-tax-advantaged account that supports both health and wealth.

Long-Term Care Insurance

Long-term care insurance can help cover expenses related to extended care, whether in a nursing facility, assisted living, or at home. Given the high cost of long-term care, insurance can alleviate the financial burden on you and your family. While premiums can be substantial, securing a policy early, usually in your 50s, can reduce costs.

Another option is a hybrid insurance policy that combines long-term care coverage with life insurance. This structure provides a death benefit if long-term care isn't needed, offering flexibility and value. Researching policies early and working with a financial advisor can help determine if this coverage aligns with your financial goals.

Long-term care insurance protects both your assets and your peace of mind.

Medicare and Supplemental Coverage

Medicare is a critical part of retirement planning in the U.S., but it doesn't cover all expenses. Supplemental insurance plans, such as Medigap, can help fill in the gaps by covering costs like copayments, deductibles, and other out-of-pocket expenses. Evaluating your healthcare needs and budget helps you choose the right Medicare plan and supplemental coverage, ensuring comprehensive healthcare protection.

As healthcare costs continue to rise, investing in supplemental coverage can safeguard your finances, making it easier to handle unexpected medical expenses without disrupting your lifestyle.

Planning for healthcare ensures a financially secure retirement.

Building a Legacy Through Philanthropy and Giving

Giving back is a powerful way to extend your legacy beyond wealth.

As you achieve financial independence, you may wish to use your success to support causes or communities you care about.

Philanthropy can be a fulfilling way to make a lasting impact, whether through regular donations, volunteer work, or establishing a foundation. Giving doesn't have to be on a large scale to make a difference; even small, consistent contributions can create positive change.

Consider creating a charitable giving plan that outlines how much you'll donate, what causes you'll support, and whether you want to contribute financially, with your time, or both. If you prefer a tax-advantaged approach, look into donor-advised funds (DAFs). DAFs allow you to donate assets, receive an immediate tax deduction, and distribute the funds to charities over time, giving you flexibility and control.

Philanthropy is a meaningful way to extend your legacy and make a positive impact.

Passing Down Financial Knowledge

Sharing knowledge creates a legacy that lives beyond wealth.

Passing down financial knowledge is one of the most impactful ways to support future generations. By teaching loved ones about budgeting, investing, and responsible spending, you equip them with skills that can benefit them for a lifetime. Sharing your journey to financial independence, including the lessons you learned, helps them understand the importance of patience, discipline, and resilience.

Consider hosting regular family discussions about finances or setting up a family financial education plan. These sessions could cover essential topics like saving, investing, debt management, and even estate planning basics. Providing younger family members with books, articles, or resources tailored to their age and experience level can also help build a strong foundation in personal finance.

Financial education is a legacy that empowers future generations.

Staying Adaptable to Life Changes

Flexibility is key to sustaining financial independence.

Financial independence doesn't mean life will be free of surprises or changes. Adapting to new circumstances, whether expected or unexpected, is essential for maintaining long-term stability. This adaptability includes revisiting your financial goals and adjusting your plans as needed to remain aligned with your priorities and values.

Reassessing Financial Goals Periodically

Life events—such as marriage, having children, career changes, or retirement—often impact your financial goals. Regularly reviewing and adjusting your financial plan keeps it relevant and ensures it supports your current life stage. For instance, you may want to update your retirement contributions, adjust investment allocations, or set up new savings goals as your needs evolve.

Many AI-driven financial planning tools provide annual or semi-annual reviews, which can help you see how well you're tracking toward your goals. These tools also offer recommendations based on changes in your income, expenses, or investments, making it easier to adapt your plan as circumstances shift.

Regular financial check-ins keep your goals current and your path clear.

Adapting Investment Strategies

Your investment strategy should reflect your financial needs, risk tolerance, and timeline, all of which can change over time. Early in your journey, you might prioritize growth by investing in higher-risk assets, while later, a conservative approach may be preferable to preserve wealth.

As you approach or enter retirement, consider reducing exposure to volatile assets and increasing allocations to stable investments, such as bonds, dividend-paying stocks, or real estate. AI-powered platforms can automate these adjustments based on your retirement timeline, making it simple to maintain an investment strategy that aligns with your current stage of life.

Adapting investments keeps your portfolio balanced and aligned with your needs.

Preparing for Legacy and End-of-Life Planning

Preparing for the future ensures that your wishes are respected.

End-of-life planning might not be a pleasant topic, but it's an important part of responsible financial management. It allows you to specify your wishes, minimize burdens on loved ones, and ensure a smooth transition of assets. An end-of-life plan can include advance directives, funeral arrangements, and instructions for the handling of personal belongings.

Creating a "legacy file" or "family binder" with essential documents, account information, and instructions provides clarity for your family and loved ones. This file should include key contacts, login credentials, insurance policies, estate planning documents, and any specific instructions you want to leave. Updating this file regularly ensures it remains accurate and comprehensive.

An end-of-life plan brings peace of mind and clarity for loved ones.

Final Thoughts on Securing Lasting Financial Independence

Financial independence is a journey that evolves with you.

Achieving financial independence is a remarkable accomplishment, but securing it requires a commitment to lifelong learning, adaptability, and forward-thinking. By planning for retirement, preparing for healthcare costs, building a legacy, and remaining adaptable, you create a future that is both financially stable and fulfilling.

Throughout this journey, remember that financial independence isn't just about numbers—it's about creating a life that aligns with your values, supports your loved ones, and leaves a positive impact. With careful planning and the right mindset, financial independence can be a source of freedom, resilience, and joy that extends far beyond your own lifetime.

Financial independence is more than a goal; it's a legacy that shapes the future.

Chapter – 11:
Evolving with Financial Independence – Adapting to Life's Changes

Financial independence is a dynamic journey that evolves as life unfolds.

Achieving financial independence is a significant milestone, yet it's only part of a larger, ongoing process. As you move through different life stages, your priorities, goals, and even financial landscape may change. Financial independence gives you the freedom to navigate these changes with confidence, but staying aligned with your evolving needs requires periodic adjustments, flexibility, and self-reflection.

In this chapter, we'll explore strategies for adapting to new phases in life, responding to economic shifts, and ensuring that your financial independence remains resilient and fulfilling over time.

True financial independence adapts to support each stage of your life.

Embracing New Life Phases with Flexibility

Every life stage brings new priorities and adjustments.

As you progress through life, major events and transitions—such as marriage, starting a family, career shifts, and retirement—can impact your financial priorities. Embracing these changes with a flexible approach helps you maintain financial stability and satisfaction as your life evolves.

Marriage and Partnership

Marriage or long-term partnership often brings new financial dynamics, including joint expenses, shared goals, and the potential for combining assets. Clear, open communication about finances is essential in any partnership, whether you decide to merge finances fully, keep separate accounts, or use a hybrid approach.

Set up regular "money dates" with your partner to review finances, discuss shared goals, and address any concerns. Developing a joint financial plan that respects both partners' values helps ensure that financial independence supports your relationship and mutual aspirations.

Communication is the cornerstone of shared financial independence.

Starting a Family

Starting a family brings new financial considerations, from healthcare and education expenses to lifestyle adjustments and the need for financial security. Revisiting your budget, insurance needs, and savings targets allows you to make room for these changes without compromising your financial independence.

For instance, setting up a college fund early on can provide a head start in saving for education expenses. Tax-advantaged accounts, like 529 plans in the U.S., offer benefits that make saving for a child's education more efficient.

Adapting your financial plan ensures that family life aligns with financial independence.

Career Transitions

Career changes, whether by choice or circumstance, often impact your income, lifestyle, and financial goals. If you're considering a career shift, either for personal fulfillment or higher income, planning ahead financially will allow you to navigate the transition smoothly. For example, building an emergency fund or setting aside a "transition fund" provides a financial cushion as you adjust to the new role.

For those achieving financial independence early, the flexibility to pursue work based on passion rather than necessity is a major advantage. Financial independence allows you to consider part-time, freelance, or entrepreneurial ventures that align with personal interests, even if they offer a lower salary.

Financial independence turns career choices into opportunities for growth and fulfillment.

Navigating Economic Shifts and Market Volatility

Staying calm in a changing economic landscape is essential for lasting independence.

Financial independence doesn't shield you entirely from economic changes or market volatility. Economic downturns, inflation, and market corrections can influence your investments, expenses, and financial outlook. However, by maintaining a resilient and diversified financial plan, you can weather these changes with confidence.

Reviewing and Rebalancing Investments

Market fluctuations may require you to review and rebalance your investment portfolio periodically. Diversification helps protect against significant losses in any one area, but it's also important to adjust asset allocations based on your current life phase and risk tolerance.

For example, during a market downturn, avoid making hasty decisions to sell off investments at a loss. Instead, consider the potential for recovery and maintain a long-term perspective. Rebalancing your portfolio—by adjusting the proportion of stocks, bonds, and other assets—ensures that your investments remain aligned with your financial needs and risk tolerance.

Staying disciplined during market shifts protects your financial foundation.

Adapting to Inflation and Rising Costs

Inflation, or the gradual rise in prices, can erode the purchasing power of your money over time. If inflation rates are high, consider adjusting your budget to account for increased expenses, especially in categories like housing, food, and healthcare. Investing in assets that historically outpace inflation, such as stocks or real estate, helps mitigate its impact on your long-term savings.

Building inflation protection into your financial plan ensures that rising costs won't undermine your financial independence. Adjusting your investment strategy to include inflation-resistant assets provides additional security as you navigate an evolving economy.

Adaptability to inflation maintains the stability of your financial independence.

Maintaining a Vision-Aligned Financial Plan

Your financial plan should evolve to support your changing vision.

Financial independence gives you the freedom to live in alignment with your values and priorities, but these can shift over time. What might have been essential in one phase of life may become less relevant or be replaced by new interests and ambitions. Revisiting your financial plan periodically to ensure it reflects your current vision and goals is key to maintaining satisfaction and purpose.

For instance, if your priorities shift toward travel, giving back, or learning new skills, adjust your budget and savings targets to accommodate these interests. Likewise, as your needs for security and stability evolve, you may choose to allocate more resources toward conservative investments or charitable giving.

Keeping your plan in tune with your values enriches the journey of financial independence.

Adjusting for Lifestyle Changes

Financial independence means having the flexibility to adapt your lifestyle as you grow.

As you experience life's shifts, your vision for financial independence may evolve. Major lifestyle changes—such as relocating, scaling down, or even upscaling in retirement—can affect your financial requirements and priorities. By maintaining flexibility, you can modify your plan to reflect these changes while staying aligned with what matters most to you.

Downsizing or Upscaling in Retirement

Once you reach financial independence, particularly in retirement, you may consider lifestyle changes like downsizing to simplify and reduce costs, or even upscaling if you want to experience more luxuries. Downsizing—such as moving to a smaller home or a region with a lower cost of living—can free up capital, reduce expenses, and make your money last longer.

Conversely, if you're financially secure, you may want to invest in experiences or upgrade certain aspects of your lifestyle. This could involve moving to a location with a better climate, traveling, or purchasing a vacation home. By regularly assessing your financial goals, you ensure that these lifestyle changes remain sustainable and fulfilling.

The freedom to adapt your lifestyle enriches the experience of financial independence.

Exploring New Passions and Interests

As financial independence provides time and resources, you might find yourself drawn to new interests or pursuits, such as volunteering, creative hobbies, or learning new skills. Integrating these passions into your financial plan allows you to explore them without compromising your long-term stability.

Consider setting aside a "passion fund" for activities that bring you joy and align with your evolving values. If, for instance, you want to start a side business or engage in more extensive travel, budgeting for these activities brings intentionality and purpose to your spending.

Your evolving interests are part of what makes financial independence dynamic and rewarding.

Building a Legacy Aligned with Your Values

Leaving a legacy is about more than wealth—it's about making a lasting impact.

Financial independence offers the opportunity to think beyond personal needs, considering how you want to contribute to others' lives or to causes you care about. Building a legacy can mean passing down financial resources, instilling values, or creating structures that continue to support your vision.

Charitable Giving and Philanthropy

If charitable giving is important to you, financial independence allows you to support meaningful causes in a way that aligns with your values. Consider creating a giving plan that allocates a percentage of your income or net worth to charity each year. Some people choose to set up donor-advised funds (DAFs), which provide tax benefits and allow for a structured approach to charitable contributions over time.

Philanthropy is not limited to financial support. Volunteering, mentoring, or using your expertise to support organizations you care about also leave a positive mark. Whether financial or personal, your contributions reflect the values you wish to pass on to future generations.

Philanthropy is a way to shape the world in line with your values.

Creating a Family Legacy

If you have children or other loved ones, leaving a family legacy involves more than passing on wealth. Teaching the next generation about financial responsibility, resilience, and the value of independence equips them to manage their finances wisely. Regular family discussions, guidance, and shared activities—such as charitable projects—reinforce the values you want to leave behind.

Consider including younger family members in your financial planning process, discussing why certain goals or values are important to you. Documenting your experiences and the principles that shaped your journey provides guidance that extends beyond material assets.

Financial independence gives you the chance to pass on both wealth and wisdom.

Cultivating a Proactive and Reflective Mindset

Financial independence thrives with a balance of proactivity and reflection.

Maintaining financial independence is not just about managing money; it's also about managing your mindset. As life progresses, regularly taking time to reflect on your financial journey and where you want to go next helps you stay connected to your goals. A proactive approach keeps your finances adaptable, ensuring they align with your evolving values and vision.

Setting Periodic Reviews

Set aside time each quarter or year to review your financial goals, track progress, and reassess your vision for financial independence. During these reviews, ask yourself questions like:

- Do my current goals still reflect what's most important to me?

- Have there been any changes in my life or interests that call for adjustments?

- What challenges have I encountered, and how can I address them?

These reviews allow you to make course corrections early, ensuring that your financial independence journey remains sustainable and satisfying.

Periodic reviews keep your journey on course, adaptable, and fulfilling.

Celebrating Progress and Reflecting on Growth

Celebrating milestones, no matter how small, reinforces your progress and builds motivation. Acknowledge the progress you've made—whether it's achieving a financial goal, adapting to a major life change, or cultivating a new habit. Celebrating reminds you that financial independence isn't just about reaching a final destination but about enjoying each phase of the journey.

Additionally, reflecting on your growth helps you appreciate the lessons learned and the resilience built along the way. By recognizing how far you've come, you stay motivated and open to whatever lies ahead.

Celebration and reflection enrich your financial independence journey.

Embracing the Freedom to Redefine Goals

Financial independence allows you to pursue new dreams, again and again.

The true beauty of financial independence lies in its adaptability. As your life changes, so can your vision for the future. The freedom to redefine goals allows you to pursue new dreams, discover new passions, and prioritize what brings you joy and fulfillment at any stage of life. This flexibility ensures that financial independence remains an enriching experience rather than a static endpoint.

For example, after achieving a certain level of wealth or financial security, you may decide to focus more on creative pursuits, explore new hobbies, or even start a new career. Financial independence grants you the flexibility to make these decisions without the constraints of financial necessity.

Redefining your goals keeps financial independence meaningful and vibrant.

Final Thoughts on Adapting to Life's Changes

Financial independence is a lifelong journey of growth and change.

Financial independence is not a rigid goal but a dynamic journey that adapts with each new phase of life. By embracing flexibility, reflecting on your values, and adjusting your plan as you grow, you ensure that your financial freedom supports a life that is deeply aligned with who you are and what you aspire to be.

As you continue on this journey, remember that financial independence empowers you not only to secure your future but also to shape it according to your dreams and priorities. Embrace the changes, welcome new possibilities, and let your financial freedom evolve alongside you.

The journey of financial independence is an ever-evolving story of growth, resilience, and fulfillment.

Chapter – 12:
The Future of AI in Personal Finance

AI is transforming personal finance, creating new paths to financial independence.

Artificial Intelligence (AI) is no longer just a tool for large corporations or high-net-worth investors. Today, AI-powered applications have become accessible to individuals of all financial backgrounds, offering personalized insights, automation, and advanced financial planning capabilities that make managing personal finances simpler and more effective. As AI continues to advance, its role in personal finance will only grow, creating more opportunities for people to achieve and sustain financial independence.

This chapter explores the future of AI in personal finance, examining how upcoming technologies will shape financial decision-making, wealth building, and financial security.

The future of AI promises greater empowerment, personalization, and financial freedom for all.

Personalized Financial Insights and Recommendations

AI tailors financial advice to your unique situation.

Traditionally, financial advice has been generalized, relying on standardized rules that don't always suit individual circumstances. However, as AI develops, it is becoming increasingly adept at delivering highly personalized financial recommendations. By analyzing vast amounts of personal data—such as spending habits, income patterns, investment history, and even lifestyle preferences—AI can provide tailored advice that aligns closely with your unique financial situation.

Hyper-Personalized Budgeting and Spending Guidance

AI budgeting tools of the future will move beyond basic categorization. They will provide real-time insights and adaptive recommendations that respond to changes in income, expenses, or life events. For instance, an AI budgeting tool may automatically adjust monthly allocations based on your recent spending patterns or notify you of potential overspending in a category based on historical trends.

Some advanced systems may even simulate how different spending decisions affect your future savings, offering proactive suggestions to help you stay on track toward long-term goals. Hyper-personalized budgeting will make financial planning both efficient and intuitive, helping you make real-time adjustments that reinforce good habits.

Personalized insights make every financial decision intentional and informed.

Adaptive Investment Portfolios

Investment management is set to undergo a significant transformation with AI. Current robo-advisors already create personalized portfolios, but future AI-driven investment platforms will take it further, adjusting portfolios dynamically as market conditions, individual goals, and risk tolerances shift. These systems will use predictive analytics to anticipate economic changes, suggest potential investment moves, and balance risk based on personal factors, like age, retirement goals, or financial goals.

Moreover, AI-driven platforms may soon integrate real-world data beyond just financial indicators, such as climate change impact, geopolitical events, and technological advances, allowing users to make investment choices that reflect their ethical and financial priorities. These advancements will enable AI to create portfolios that not only meet your financial objectives but also align with your personal values.

Dynamic, adaptive investments align growth with changing personal and global landscapes.

Enhanced Automation for Effortless Money Management

Automation is transforming financial independence from effort-intensive to effortless.

Automation is already streamlining tasks like bill payments and savings transfers, but the future holds even more sophisticated applications. Future AI systems will be able to manage complex, multi-layered financial activities with little to no input from the user, going beyond single tasks to automate entire financial processes.

Automatic Savings and Expense Management

Future AI-driven systems will not only automate savings but will also optimize the amounts saved based on your spending patterns, upcoming expenses, and future financial goals. For example, if an AI system detects a surplus in your monthly cash flow, it could automatically allocate additional funds to investment accounts or long-term savings goals. Similarly, during months when expenses rise, the system might adjust savings contributions temporarily to maintain cash flow.

This level of automation could extend to managing subscriptions, identifying unused services, and canceling them on your behalf. By reducing wasteful spending and ensuring consistent savings, AI will make it easier to maximize wealth without requiring constant attention.

Effortless savings automation helps you stay financially resilient with minimal effort.

Streamlined Tax Optimization and Planning

Tax planning is a complex yet essential part of financial independence, and future AI technology will significantly simplify this process. AI-driven tax planning tools will analyze transactions in real-time, identifying potential tax deductions, credits, and optimization strategies as they happen, rather than only at tax season. By year-end, AI could provide a detailed breakdown of your taxable income, making it easier to take advantage of deductions and avoid unexpected tax liabilities.

In the future, advanced tax planning systems might also suggest changes to your portfolio to minimize capital gains taxes or recommend retirement contributions based on your income fluctuations. These capabilities will make tax planning an ongoing, integrated aspect of financial management, helping you keep more of what you earn.

AI-powered tax optimization ensures you maximize earnings while minimizing tax obligations.

Proactive Financial Health Monitoring and Alerts

Financial health monitoring becomes real-time and proactive.

The future of AI in personal finance will also include proactive monitoring of your financial health. Much like health trackers that monitor vital signs, AI-driven financial tools will continuously assess key indicators—like cash flow, debt levels, investment performance, and credit scores. These tools will alert you to potential issues, offer corrective actions, and keep you informed about opportunities to improve your financial health.

For example, if the system detects that you are close to reaching a debt threshold, it might alert you and suggest adjustments to your spending or a strategy for faster repayment. Likewise, if an opportunity arises to refinance a loan at a lower rate, the AI might notify you and provide a cost-benefit analysis.

Real-time financial monitoring ensures you stay in control, no matter how complex your finances.

AI and Behavioral Finance – Encouraging Good Financial Habits

AI reinforces positive financial behaviors through tailored feedback.

Behavioral finance studies how emotions and biases affect financial decisions. Future AI systems will integrate principles of behavioral finance, providing tailored feedback that encourages responsible habits and discourages impulsive spending. For instance, if an AI tool detects frequent discretionary spending, it could gently remind you of your savings goals, creating a subtle nudge to help you stay focused on priorities.

AI-driven financial tools could also implement gamification, turning financial milestones into rewarding achievements. By offering rewards, progress indicators, and motivational messages, AI can make financial planning more engaging, helping you sustain positive financial behaviors over the long term.

Behavioral finance in AI transforms financial management into a rewarding experience.

Privacy and Ethical Considerations in AI-Driven Personal Finance

As AI advances, privacy and ethics become paramount.

With AI gaining access to sensitive financial data, maintaining privacy and ethical use is critical. Responsible AI development will prioritize transparency, giving users control over their data and how it's used. Companies will need to ensure that data is encrypted, anonymized where possible, and used only for the purposes of improving financial management and achieving the user's goals.

Furthermore, as AI-driven systems become more capable of making autonomous financial decisions, there's a growing need for ethical oversight to prevent bias, discrimination, or unintentional consequences. Future AI tools in personal finance will ideally include ethical guidelines, with companies making their algorithms transparent and accessible to foster trust.

AI must prioritize privacy and ethics, empowering users without compromising security.

Final Thoughts on AI's Role in Financial Independence

AI empowers a future of financial independence defined by accessibility, ease, and personal growth.

AI in personal finance is evolving from a tool for convenience to an essential partner in achieving financial independence. As AI continues to advance, it promises a future where everyone, regardless of financial knowledge or background, can access high-quality financial guidance, make informed investment decisions, and maintain financial stability with minimal effort.

With personalized insights, seamless automation, proactive monitoring, and ethical considerations at the forefront, AI in personal finance will shape a world where financial independence is not just achievable but sustainable. Embrace these technologies as allies on your journey, knowing that the future of AI-driven personal finance is one of empowerment, flexibility, and enduring freedom.

The future of AI in personal finance holds endless possibilities for a life of security, freedom, and purpose.

Chapter – 13:
Taking Control of Your Financial Destiny

Financial independence is within your reach—take the first step toward a life of freedom.

Achieving financial independence isn't just about accumulating wealth; it's about creating a life that aligns with your values, empowers you to pursue your passions, and provides security and freedom. Throughout this journey, you've learned the essential steps to make that vision a reality—from budgeting and saving to investing and building a resilient mindset. In this final chapter, we'll review these core concepts, provide actionable steps to help you take charge, and offer encouragement as you move forward with confidence.

Recap of Key Concepts

1. **Setting a Strong Financial Foundation** – The journey began with understanding the importance of budgeting, managing expenses, and saving consistently. These foundational steps provide the clarity and discipline needed to direct resources toward long-term goals.

2. **Building a Diversified Income Stream** – Relying on a single income source is risky. Through freelancing, side hustles, investments, and passive income strategies, diversifying your income reduces dependency and accelerates your path to financial freedom.

3. **Investing for Growth** – Investing isn't just for the wealthy; it's a powerful tool that allows your money to grow over time. Learning about stocks, bonds, mutual funds, real estate, and ETFs—along with the importance of a diversified portfolio— enables you to build wealth in a sustainable way.

4. **The Power of Automation and AI** – Embracing technology helps streamline your financial management. Automated savings, budgeting apps, and robo-advisors reduce the time and effort needed to keep your finances in order, making financial independence more accessible.

5. **Building a Resilient Mindset** – Financial independence requires mental strength and resilience. Developing patience, discipline, and adaptability keeps you grounded through challenges, ensuring you stay committed to your goals.

6. **Planning for the Long Term** – Preparing for retirement, creating an estate plan, and securing healthcare coverage are all steps that support a stable, independent future. Effective long-term planning allows you to enjoy peace of mind and freedom, knowing you've prepared for life's changes.

7. **The Future of AI in Personal Finance** – The advancements in AI-driven personal finance tools mean that financial independence is increasingly accessible. With personalized insights, automation, and real-time monitoring, AI empowers you to make informed decisions and adapt to new opportunities effortlessly.

Taking Action: Steps to Empower Your Financial Future

1. Define Your Vision of Financial Independence

   o Write down what financial independence looks like for you. Is it the freedom to travel, the ability to pursue creative passions, or the security to retire early? Understanding your "why" helps anchor your motivation and guides your decisions.

2. Create a Financial Roadmap

   o Start with a clear financial roadmap that outlines your goals. Include short-term goals (building an emergency fund, paying off debt) and long-term goals (retirement savings, investments). Break down these goals into actionable steps with timelines, so you have a path to follow.

3. Automate Your Savings and Investments

   o Automation is a powerful tool that keeps your financial plan moving forward without requiring constant attention. Set up automatic transfers to savings accounts, retirement funds, or investment platforms. This "pay yourself first" approach prioritizes your goals and builds wealth effortlessly over time.

4. Invest in Your Financial Education

   o Commit to continuous learning about personal finance. Follow trusted finance blogs, read books on investing, and keep up with market trends. As you learn more, you'll feel empowered to make informed decisions and adapt to new opportunities.

5. Track Your Progress Regularly

   o Schedule regular financial reviews to track your progress. Use budgeting apps, investment platforms, or even a simple spreadsheet to see how you're advancing toward your goals. These check-ins allow you to celebrate wins, make adjustments, and stay motivated.

6. Diversify Your Income Sources

   o Explore ways to diversify your income. Whether through a side hustle, freelancing, or investing, building multiple income streams provides security and accelerates your progress. Choose income opportunities that align with your skills and interests, making it easier to maintain.

7. Prepare for the Long Term with Estate and Retirement Planning

   o Financial independence isn't just for today; it's about securing your future. Create or update an estate plan, consider life insurance, and ensure your retirement accounts are on track. These steps will provide a lasting legacy for you and your loved ones.

8. Leverage AI and Technology for Financial Management

   o Use AI-driven tools to optimize budgeting, investments, and savings. Personal finance apps, robo-advisors, and automated tax planning tools reduce the complexity of financial management, allowing you to focus on big-picture goals.

Overcoming Common Challenges

Challenges will arise—approach them with resilience and a growth mindset.

1. **Setbacks and Unexpected Expenses** – An unexpected expense or temporary setback can feel discouraging. Build an emergency fund to cover unexpected costs and view setbacks as temporary. Each challenge is a learning opportunity that strengthens your journey.

2. **Staying Motivated** – Financial independence is a long-term goal that requires persistence. Regularly revisit your vision to stay inspired, celebrate small wins, and surround yourself with supportive communities or mentors who encourage your journey.

3. **Dealing with Market Volatility** – Market fluctuations are inevitable, but maintaining a long-term investment perspective helps you weather economic changes. Diversification, discipline, and a commitment to your goals will keep your investments on course.

Final Words of Encouragement

Financial independence is a life of freedom, security, and choice.

The journey you're on isn't just about reaching a number in your bank account. It's about building a life that aligns with your dreams, free from the constraints of financial worry. Financial independence empowers you to live intentionally, explore passions, and contribute to the world in ways that bring fulfillment. Embrace this journey with confidence, knowing that every step forward—no matter how small—brings you closer to a life of freedom and purpose.

Remember that financial independence is unique to each individual. The pace, strategies, and goals are yours to shape. Stay true to your values, adapt as you grow, and continue learning. Financial independence isn't an endpoint; it's a way of living that reflects your goals, priorities, and values.

You hold the power to take control of your financial destiny. Start today, stay committed, and embrace the journey toward a future filled with freedom, security, and limitless potential.

About the Author
Dr. Cedric B. Howard

With nearly three decades of experience in higher education as a senior level executive, I am honored to be recognized as a pivotal figure in the field. Over the years, I've remained steadfast in my commitment to both my students and colleagues, striving to make a meaningful difference in their lives. My passion for education has allowed me to contribute significantly to the academic world, earning me the respect and admiration of many along the way.

But my journey extends beyond the classroom. I have had the privilege of managing projects in various industries, honing skills that have allowed me to bring practical, real-world experience to my work. This diverse background has shaped my perspective and broadened my ability to inspire and lead in multiple arenas.

One of the initiatives I'm most proud of is my work in financial literacy. In the early 2000s, I created a financial literacy curriculum designed to empower young adults, particularly those in college, to become financially independent. This wasn't just about teaching numbers; it was about equipping the next generation with the tools to take control of their financial futures. Along the way, I also developed workshops to guide students through the real-life application of these principles, ensuring they had the knowledge and confidence to make sound financial decisions.

This book is a reflection of that same curriculum. It's a collection of the foundational principles that I've spent years refining, a culmination of my passion for helping others build a secure and independent future. Through this book, my hope is to continue to inspire and empower individuals on their journey toward financial literacy and beyond.